The Amazing Animals of Kenya and Tanzania

A Journey Through the Region's Most Spectacular Wildlife

Copyright © 2023, Ursula Lina Velez.

All rights reserved. No part of this publication may be reproduced, distributed, or transmitted in any form or by any means, including photocopying, recording, or other electronic or mechanical methods, without the prior written permission of the publisher, except in the case of brief quotations embodied in critical reviews and certain other noncommercial uses permitted by copyright law. This book was created with the help of Artificial Intelligence technology to enhance the writing process.

The information contained in this book is for entertainment purposes only. The author and publisher of this book are not responsible for any damages or consequences arising from the use of this book's content. While every effort has been made to provide accurate and up-to-date information, readers are advised to consult with professional advisors in the relevant fields concerning any information or advice contained in this book.

All pictures used in this content are sourced from Canva and are considered license-free. Canva provides a platform that offers a variety of images that can be used for personal and commercial purposes without infringing on any copyright restrictions. The use of Canva images in this context is in compliance with Canva's terms of service and licensing agreements.

Introduction 6

The Majestic Maasai Lion: King of the Savannah 8

The Enigmatic African Elephant: Gentle Giants 10

Leopards of the Twilight: Shadows in the Grass 12

Cheetahs: The Speedsters of the Serengeti 14

The Great Wildebeest Migration: A Spectacle of Survival 16

The Rhinoceros: Armor of the Wilderness 18

Giraffes: Sentinels of the Savanna 21

Hippo Havens: Giants of the Rivers 24

African Buffalo: The Formidable Bovines 27

Zebras: Patterns in the Plains 30

The Baboon Troops: Societies in the Trees 33

Warthogs: Wonders of the Wild 36

The Dainty Dik-Dik: Tiny Titans 39

Flamingo Flocks: A Dance in Pink 42

The Ostrich: Sprinters of the Savannah 45

Crocodiles: Stealthy Predators of the Waterways 48

The Antelopes of Amboseli: Grace in Motion 51

Hyenas: The Misunderstood Scavengers 54

The Vervet Monkey: A Prankster's Life 57

Mongoose: The Snakes' Nemesis 60

Bushbabies: The Nocturnal Acrobats 63

The African Wild Dog: Endangered Hunters 66

Servals: The Silent Stalkers 69

Pangolins: Scaled Mysteries of the Night 72

The Secretary Bird: Stalking the Savannah 75

The Caracal: Elegance in Stealth 78

The Honey Badger: Fierce and Fearless 81

The Bat-Eared Fox: Unseen Nighttime Forager 84

Colobus Monkeys: The Treetop Philosophers 87

Porcupines: The Prickly Wanderers 90

The African Fish Eagle: Ruler of the Skies 93

Aardvark: Oddities of the African Bush 96

The Bushpig: Kenya's Wild Swine 99

The Martial Eagle: The Aerial Predator 101

Pelicans of the Rift Valley: Masters of the Water 103

The African Python: Silent Giant of the Savannah 106

The Nile Monitor: River Sentinel 108

Jackals: The Opportunistic Omnivores 110

The Ground Hornbill: The Ground-Dwelling Avian 113

The African Civet: The Nocturnal Forager 116

The Servaline Genet: Kenya's Elusive Carnivore 118

Epilogue: Reflections on Kenya and Tanzania's Wildlife Tapestry 120

Introduction

The Heartbeat of Africa: A Journey into the Wild
Welcome to a journey that transcends the ordinary, a voyage into the heart of Africa's wild heartlands - Kenya and Tanzania. These lands, rich in history, culture, and biodiversity, are the setting for our exploration of some of the world's most fascinating wildlife. This book, an ode to the natural wonders of these countries, is more than just a catalogue of animals; it is a tribute to the resilience and beauty of life in its most primal form.

The Landscapes of Kenya and Tanzania
Kenya and Tanzania are countries of immense geographical diversity, offering a range of habitats from the snow-capped peaks of Mount Kenya and Kilimanjaro to the vast savannahs of the Maasai Mara and Serengeti. The Great Rift Valley, a geological marvel, runs through both countries, adding to the dramatic landscapes that form the backdrop to our narrative. These habitats are not just picturesque sceneries; they are vital ecosystems that support a plethora of life forms.

A Symphony of Ecosystems
In these ecosystems, every species plays a crucial role. The grasslands of the savannah, dotted with acacia trees, are not just home to the iconic African Big Five (lion, elephant, buffalo, leopard, and rhinoceros) but also to a myriad of other species, each contributing to the ecological balance. The wetlands and rivers, teeming with hippos and crocodiles, are lifelines in the arid landscapes, while the dense forests provide refuge to elusive creatures like the African wild dogs and bushbabies.

A Dynamic Interplay
Predator and prey, flora and fauna, the cycle of life and death – these natural processes form the core of the ecological tapestry. The Great Wildebeest Migration, a spectacle of life and survival, epitomizes this dynamic interplay. Millions of wildebeest, accompanied by zebras and gazelles, traverse the plains in search of fresh pasture, braving predators and treacherous river crossings. This annual journey is not just a display of endurance but a testament to the interconnectedness of life.

Conservation: A Fragile Balance
The wildlife of Kenya and Tanzania is under threat from various fronts – habitat loss, climate change, poaching, and human-wildlife conflict. Conservation efforts are critical in ensuring the survival of these species. Protected areas like national parks and reserves play a pivotal role, but conservation is a complex issue that requires the involvement of local communities and international support. This book aims to highlight not only the beauty and majesty of these animals but also the challenges they face in their fight for survival.

Cultural Connections
The animals of Kenya and Tanzania are deeply intertwined with the cultures and traditions of the local communities. For many tribes, like the Maasai, wildlife is an integral part of their heritage and identity. These animals are not just passive inhabitants of the land but are central to the stories, beliefs, and livelihoods of the people who share their home.

Embarking on the Journey
As we delve into the chapters of this book, each dedicated to a different animal, we invite you to immerse yourself in the wonders of Kenya and Tanzania's wildlife. From the stealthy leopard to the humble dik-dik, each animal has a story to tell – a story of adaptation, survival, and coexistence.
In this exploration, we not only celebrate the marvels of nature but also acknowledge our responsibility to protect and preserve these treasures for future generations. Let this book be a window into the soul of Africa, a glimpse into the lives of its most remarkable inhabitants, and a call to action to safeguard the natural legacy of our planet.

The Majestic Maasai Lion: King of the Savannah

A Regal Presence
In the vast expanses of Kenya and Tanzania's savannah, a distinct roar cuts through the dawn and dusk, a sound that resonates with the very essence of the African wilds. It belongs to the Maasai lion, a symbol of strength, courage, and majesty. This chapter delves into the world of this magnificent creature, exploring its biology, behavior, and the challenges it faces in the modern world.

The Biology of the Maasai Lion
The Maasai lion, a subspecies of the African lion, is distinguished by its impressive size and magnificent mane, which ranges in color from golden to black. Males, larger than females, can weigh up to 250 kilograms (550 pounds) and grow up to 4 meters (13 feet) in length, including the tail. Their powerful physique is a testament to their role as top predators, but it is their social structure that truly sets them apart in the animal kingdom.

Social Structure and Behavior

Lions are the most social of all big cats, living in groups known as prides. A typical pride consists of around 15 members, including several adult females, their young, and a few males. The females, often related, are the core of the pride and are responsible for hunting and rearing the cubs. Males, usually brothers or coalition partners, protect the pride's territory.

Hunting is a cooperative endeavor in lion prides, with females working together to outmaneuver their prey. Despite their size and strength, lions have a relatively low hunting success rate, and teamwork is crucial for their survival.

Communication and Behavior

Lions communicate through a complex system of vocalizations, body language, and scent marking. The iconic roar, audible up to 8 kilometers (5 miles) away, is used to proclaim territory and locate other pride members. Whisker spots and tail flicks are among the subtle cues they use to signal intentions and emotions to each other.

The Role in the Ecosystem

As apex predators, Maasai lions play a crucial role in the savannah ecosystem. They help maintain the balance by preying on herbivores, thus preventing overgrazing. This predatory role ensures the health and diversity of the grassland habitat.

Challenges and Conservation

The Maasai lion faces numerous threats, including habitat loss due to human encroachment, conflicts with livestock owners, and diseases like canine distemper and bovine tuberculosis. Additionally, the illegal wildlife trade poses a significant threat to lion populations.

Conservation efforts involve habitat protection, conflict mitigation strategies, and community-based conservation programs. National parks and reserves in Kenya and Tanzania, such as the Maasai Mara and Serengeti, provide critical sanctuaries for these lions.

Cultural Significance

For the Maasai people, the lion holds great cultural significance. Traditionally, killing a lion was a rite of passage for young warriors, though this practice has diminished due to conservation efforts. Today, the Maasai lion remains a symbol of strength and pride, both for the local communities and for all who marvel at the wonders of the African savannah.

The Enigmatic African Elephant: Gentle Giants

The Quintessence of Africa's Wildlife
The African elephant, a majestic and enigmatic creature, reigns as one of the most iconic symbols of the African wilderness. This chapter unveils the life, habits, and challenges of these gentle giants, focusing on their presence in Kenya and Tanzania, where they play a crucial role in the ecosystem and culture.

A Tale of Two Species
There are two species of African elephants: the larger savannah elephant and the smaller, more elusive forest elephant. The savannah elephants, primarily found in Kenya and Tanzania, are the largest land mammals on Earth. Males can weigh up to 6,000 kilograms (13,000 pounds) and stand up to 4 meters (13 feet) at the shoulder. Their remarkable size is matched by their distinctive features: large ears that resemble the African continent and long, curved tusks.

Family Structure and Social Life
Elephants are profoundly social creatures, forming complex matriarchal societies. Herds are typically led by an older female, the matriarch, and consist of her daughters, sisters, and their offspring. The social bonds among them are strong, with communication playing a vital role in their daily lives.

Elephant communication is sophisticated, involving a range of vocalizations, from trumpets to low-frequency rumbles inaudible to humans. These sounds facilitate long-distance communication and play a significant role in their social interactions and coordination.

The Keystone of the Ecosystem
As ecosystem engineers, elephants have a significant impact on their environment. Their feeding habits, which include uprooting trees and stripping bark, shape the savannah and forest landscapes. This behavior creates microhabitats for other species and is crucial for seed dispersal and germination, making elephants vital for the biodiversity of their habitats.

Intelligence and Emotion
Elephants are renowned for their intelligence and emotional depth. They exhibit behaviors indicative of empathy, grief, and even self-awareness. Their memory, particularly regarding locations of water sources, is critical for survival in the harsh African landscapes.

Human-Elephant Conflict and Conservation Challenges
With the expansion of human settlements and agriculture, human-elephant conflict has become a significant issue. Elephants often raid crops, leading to confrontations with farmers. Poaching for ivory is another grave threat, leading to drastic declines in elephant populations.

Conservation efforts are multifaceted, involving anti-poaching measures, habitat conservation, and community-based initiatives to mitigate human-elephant conflicts. Organizations and governments work to create elephant corridors to ensure safe migration routes and protect their habitats.

Cultural and Symbolic Importance
In many African cultures, elephants are revered and hold significant symbolic value. They symbolize wisdom, strength, and are often associated with good fortune. In Kenya and Tanzania, they are a cornerstone of the tourism industry, attracting visitors from all over the world, eager to witness these gentle giants in their natural habitat.

Leopards of the Twilight: Shadows in the Grass

Masters of Camouflage and Stealth
The African leopard, a creature of beauty and mystery, is the embodiment of feline grace and stealth. This chapter explores the secretive life of the leopard in Kenya and Tanzania, delving into its behavior, habitat, and the challenges it faces in the wild.

Anatomy of Elegance
The leopard is renowned for its striking coat, covered in rosettes and spots that provide excellent camouflage in various habitats. Weighing between 30 to 90 kilograms (66 to 198 pounds), they are the smallest of the 'big cats' in the genus Panthera. Despite their size, leopards are incredibly strong, capable of dragging prey much heavier than themselves up into trees.

A Solitary Existence
Leopards are solitary animals, with both males and females establishing their own territories. These territories are marked by scratching trees, leaving feces, and spraying urine. Males usually have larger territories that overlap with those of several females. The solitary nature of leopards is a stark contrast to the social structure of lions and hyenas, with whom they share their habitats.

Habitat and Adaptability
Leopards are highly adaptable and can thrive in a range of environments, from savannah and woodland to mountainous regions. Their ability to adapt has allowed them to survive in areas where other big cats have struggled. In Kenya and Tanzania, they are often found in protected areas, but they can also be spotted in more populated regions, demonstrating their versatile nature.

Hunting and Diet
Leopards are apex predators and are known for their opportunistic hunting style. They feed on a diverse diet that includes birds, rodents, and even large ungulates. Their hunting strategy is a blend of patience and stealth, often ambushing their prey followed by a burst of speed. The ability to climb trees allows them to safeguard their catch from scavengers.

Reproduction and Offspring
The gestation period for leopards is approximately 100 days, after which the female gives birth to a litter of usually two or three cubs. The mother is fiercely protective of her offspring, hiding them in dense vegetation or caves to safeguard them from predators, including other leopards. Cubs stay with their mother for about 18 to 24 months, learning crucial survival skills.

Conservation Status and Threats
Leopards face several threats, including habitat loss, poaching for their beautiful coats, and conflict with humans. These factors have led to a decline in leopard populations in some areas. Their elusive nature makes them difficult to study and protect, but conservation efforts are ongoing. Anti-poaching patrols, habitat conservation, and community awareness programs are key strategies in leopard conservation.

Leopards in Culture and Folklore
In African folklore, the leopard is often revered as a symbol of wisdom and strength. Its image is used in rituals, storytelling, and art, highlighting its significance in the cultural landscape. The leopard's ability to move silently and unseen has also given it a mystical status, often associated with the spirit world in local beliefs.

The Leopard's Place in the Ecosystem
As top predators, leopards play a crucial role in maintaining the balance of the ecosystems in which they live. By controlling the populations of their prey, they help keep a healthy balance in the food web. Their role in the ecosystem underscores the importance of their conservation for the overall health of the environment.

Cheetahs: The Speedsters of the Serengeti

Embodiment of Speed and Grace
In the sprawling savannas of the Serengeti, a remarkable creature commands attention not through its roar or size, but through its extraordinary speed and elegance. The cheetah, the fastest land animal, is an embodiment of evolutionary perfection for speed. This chapter explores the life, behavior, and challenges of the cheetahs in their natural habitat in the Serengeti.

Anatomy of the Sprinter
Cheetahs are built for speed. Their slender, streamlined body, long legs, and powerful muscles enable them to reach speeds of up to 112 km/h (70 mph). Unique among big cats, their claws are non-retractable, functioning like spikes to provide additional grip during high-speed chases. Their long tail acts as a rudder for quick and agile maneuvers.

The Art of the Hunt
Cheetahs are diurnal hunters, preferring to hunt in the early morning or late afternoon. They rely on their exceptional eyesight to spot prey and their incredible speed for short, explosive chases. Their primary prey includes small to medium-sized ungulates such as gazelles and impalas. After a chase, cheetahs need time to recover, as the high-speed pursuit takes a significant toll on their body.

Social Structure and Reproduction
Cheetahs lead a predominantly solitary life, except for females with cubs and sibling groups. Males sometimes form coalitions, usually with their brothers, to defend their territories. Females are solitary and nomadic, roaming widely. After a gestation period of around 90 days, a female cheetah gives birth to a litter of up to five cubs. The cubs are born with a mantle of long hair on their back, which helps camouflage them in the grass.

Growth and Survival of Cubs
Cheetah cubs face a high mortality rate, often falling prey to lions, hyenas, and other predators. The mother moves her cubs to new hiding places frequently to avoid detection. The cubs remain with their mother for about 18 months, learning hunting skills and how to survive in the wild.

Challenges to Survival
Cheetah populations are under threat due to habitat loss, human-wildlife conflict, and competition with other large predators. The Serengeti, however, remains one of the strongholds for cheetahs, offering a relatively safe and abundant environment. Conservation efforts include habitat preservation, research, and mitigating conflicts with humans.

Adaptations for Survival
Cheetahs have adapted various strategies to survive alongside larger predators. They often hunt during the day to avoid competition with nocturnal predators like lions and hyenas. They also consume their prey quickly and are willing to abandon it at the first sign of a threat to avoid confrontations.

The Cheetah's Place in the Ecosystem
As top predators, cheetahs play a vital role in controlling the population of their prey, thus maintaining the balance of the ecosystem. Their presence indicates a healthy, functioning ecosystem, making their conservation important not just for the species but for the Serengeti as a whole.

Cheetahs in Research and Conservation
Cheetahs are a focus for wildlife researchers, who study their behavior, genetics, and interactions with the ecosystem. These studies provide valuable insights for conservation strategies, helping to ensure that these incredible animals continue to grace the Serengeti with their presence.

The Great Wildebeest Migration: A Spectacle of Survival

A Journey of Epic Proportions
The Great Wildebeest Migration is one of the most awe-inspiring natural events on the planet. Each year, over 1.5 million wildebeest, accompanied by hundreds of thousands of zebras and gazelles, embark on a circular migration through the Serengeti-Mara ecosystem, covering over 1,800 miles. This chapter delves into the intricacies of this incredible journey, highlighting its significance and the challenges faced by these animals.

The Cycle of Life
The migration is driven by the seasonal rains and the resulting growth of grazing grass. The journey typically begins in the Ngorongoro Conservation Area in Tanzania, where the calving season starts in January and February. Here, over 500,000 calves are born within a few weeks, providing a vital start to the cycle of life that fuels the migration.

The Trek Northwards
As the dry season sets in around May, the herds start moving northwards, traversing the Grumeti River in Tanzania and eventually arriving at the Mara River, the border between Tanzania and Kenya. This journey is fraught with danger, as they encounter predators and have to cross treacherous rivers infested with crocodiles.

The Mara River Crossing

Perhaps the most dramatic element of the migration is the crossing of the Mara River. The wildebeest gather in large numbers, often hesitating for days before plunging into the water. This crossing is a perilous endeavor, with strong currents and crocodiles posing a significant threat. However, this risk is a necessary gamble for the wildebeest to reach the fertile grazing lands of the Maasai Mara.

Adaptation and Survival Strategies

The wildebeest are uniquely adapted to this migratory life. They are hardy animals, able to cover long distances and survive with minimal water. Their migratory pattern also helps rejuvenate the grasslands, as their movement and grazing patterns prevent overgrazing and allow the grasslands to recover.

The Role of Predators

Predators play a crucial role in the Great Wildebeest Migration. Lions, hyenas, leopards, and cheetahs follow the herds, taking advantage of the abundance of prey. This not only impacts the predator populations, increasing their numbers, but also ensures the health of the wildebeest population, as predators often target the weak or sick.

Human Impact and Conservation

The Great Wildebeest Migration faces challenges due to human activities. Habitat loss and fragmentation due to agricultural expansion pose a significant threat. Conservation efforts are focused on creating and maintaining protected corridors and working with local communities to ensure the sustainability of this phenomenon.

Research and Monitoring

Ongoing research and monitoring are essential to understanding the dynamics of the migration. Scientists use various methods, including satellite tracking and aerial surveys, to monitor the movement of the herds and the impact of environmental changes on the migration.

The Migration's Impact on Ecosystems

The migration is not only a spectacle of survival but also plays a vital role in shaping the ecosystems of the Serengeti and Maasai Mara. The movement of such a large number of animals impacts everything from the grasslands to the populations of predators and scavengers, making it a key component of the ecological balance in these regions.

The Rhinoceros: Armor of the Wilderness

The Embodiment of Prehistoric Majesty
The rhinoceros, a symbol of the wilderness's raw and ancient power, stands as a living relic of prehistoric times. In the landscapes of Kenya and Tanzania, two species of this majestic creature roam - the Black Rhino and the White Rhino. This chapter delves into the world of these extraordinary animals, exploring their characteristics, behavior, and the formidable challenges they face in their struggle for survival.

Distinct Species, Distinct Traits
The Black Rhino, smaller and more elusive, is known for its pointed upper lip, adapted for browsing foliage. In contrast, the larger White Rhino, with its square lip, is a grazer, feeding primarily on grass. Despite their names, both species are actually grey in color. Their thick, armor-like skin and large horns on their snouts make them one of the most recognizable creatures of the African wild.

Habitat and Lifestyle
Rhinos are generally solitary animals, with the exception of mothers and their calves. The Black Rhino inhabits bushlands and forests, using its horn and pointed lips to browse shrubs and trees. The White Rhino prefers open savannah where grass is abundant. Despite their heavy build and seemingly lethargic demeanor, rhinos can run at impressive speeds of up to 55 km/h (34 mph) and have agile maneuverability.

The Rhino's Horn: A Blessing and a Curse
A rhino's horn, made of keratin (the same material as human hair and nails), is a tool for defense, intimidation, and digging up roots and water. Unfortunately, it is also the reason behind their greatest threat - poaching. Rhino horns are highly valued in illegal wildlife trade, particularly in some Asian countries, for their supposed medicinal properties, which have no basis in scientific fact.

Behavior and Social Interaction
Rhinos are not as asocial as once thought. They have a complex social structure, communicated through vocal sounds and a wide range of postures and gestures. Their dung piles, or middens, are not just waste but also serve as a communication method, conveying age, sex, and reproductive status.

Breeding and Conservation of the Species
Rhinos have a slow reproduction rate, with females giving birth to a single calf every two to four years after a gestation period of around 16 months. This slow reproduction is a challenge for the conservation of the species, especially in the face of rampant poaching. Protecting these animals involves anti-poaching patrols, community conservation efforts, and international cooperation to curb the demand for rhino horns.

Rhinoceros in the Ecosystem
Rhinos play a crucial role in their ecosystem. Their grazing habits help shape the African landscape, creating clearings that benefit other animals. They are also important seed dispersers, aiding in the biodiversity of their habitats.

Threats Beyond Poaching
In addition to poaching, rhinos face the threat of habitat loss due to expanding human settlements and agriculture. Diseases and potential inbreeding due to isolated populations are also concerns for their conservation.

Efforts for the Future
Conservationists employ innovative strategies to protect these giants, including dehorning, translocation to safer areas, and breeding programs. Ecotourism also plays a role, providing funding and raising awareness for rhino conservation.

The Rhinoceros in Culture
In African cultures, the rhinoceros is often revered as a symbol of resilience and strength. Their portrayal in art, folklore, and literature underscores their importance not only as a keystone species but also as an integral part of Africa's cultural heritage.

Monitoring and Research
Ongoing research and monitoring are crucial in understanding the behavior, population dynamics, and health of rhinos. This scientific data informs conservation strategies and helps in the fight against the threats they face, ensuring that these armored giants continue to grace the African wilderness for generations to come.

Giraffes: Sentinels of the Savanna

Towering Elegance of the African Plains

Giraffes, with their elongated necks and towering stature, are among the most distinctive and elegant inhabitants of the African savanna. These gentle giants, the tallest land mammals on Earth, are not just a marvel of nature's design but also play a vital role in their ecosystems. This chapter explores the fascinating world of giraffes in Kenya and Tanzania, delving into their biology, behavior, and the challenges they face in the wild.

Anatomy of the Giraffe

A giraffe's height can be awe-inspiring, with males standing up to 5.5 meters (18 feet) tall and females slightly shorter. This height, largely attributed to their long necks and legs, offers them a unique advantage in both feeding and spotting predators. Interestingly, despite their long necks, giraffes have the same number of neck vertebrae as humans - seven. Each vertebra, however, is elongated and can be over 10 inches long.

Unique Physical Adaptations
Giraffes possess several unique adaptations that enable their survival. Their skin pattern, made up of complex spots, provides camouflage in the dappled light of their woodland habitats. Their long tongues, measuring up to 45 centimeters (18 inches), allow them to skillfully pluck leaves and buds from trees, especially acacia species, which form a significant part of their diet.

Giraffe Behavior and Social Structure
Giraffes are social animals, typically seen in loosely organized groups. These groupings are fluid, with members joining and leaving freely. They do not have a strict social structure, but a hierarchy can be observed, especially among males, who engage in gentle necking battles to establish dominance.

Feeding and Its Impact on the Environment
Giraffes are browsers, feeding primarily on leaves and shoots. Their feeding habits play a crucial role in shaping the savanna ecosystem. By pruning trees, they prevent overgrowth and promote new growth, which benefits other herbivores and maintains a healthy balance in the habitat.

Reproduction and Calf Rearing
Female giraffes give birth to a single calf after a gestation period of about 15 months. Calves are born tall (around 2 meters or 6 feet) and can stand and walk within a few hours of birth. The first few weeks are the most vulnerable time for a giraffe calf, as they are at risk from predators like lions and hyenas.

Challenges Facing Giraffes
Giraffes face several threats, including habitat loss due to human encroachment, poaching for their meat and hide, and environmental changes. In some areas, their populations have seen a significant decline, leading to efforts to classify certain subspecies as endangered.

Conservation Efforts
Conservation efforts for giraffes include habitat protection, anti-poaching initiatives, and research to better understand their ecology and behavior. Community involvement is also crucial, as local people play a vital role in protecting these animals and their habitats.

Giraffes in Research and Science
Scientific research on giraffes has increased in recent years, shedding light on their communication, social structures, and environmental impact. Studies have revealed that giraffes communicate at frequencies too low for humans to hear and that their populations are genetically more diverse than previously thought.

Cultural Significance of Giraffes
In African culture, giraffes are often admired for their grace and peaceful nature. They are featured in folklore and art, symbolizing intuition, flexibility, and the ability to see things from a higher perspective.

The Giraffe's Role in the Ecosystem
As key browsers in the savanna ecosystem, giraffes play an important role in nutrient cycling and vegetation management. Their presence indicates a healthy, balanced ecosystem, making their conservation crucial not only for their survival but for the overall health of the savanna.

Monitoring and Conservation Strategies
Conservationists utilize various strategies to monitor and protect giraffe populations, including aerial surveys, GPS tracking, and community-based conservation programs. These efforts are vital to ensure the survival of giraffes in their natural habitats, preserving the beauty and ecological integrity of the African savanna.

Hippo Havens: Giants of the Rivers

The River's Gentle Giants
In the waterways of Kenya and Tanzania, there lies a colossal inhabitant, often submerged, emerging as a symbol of Africa's wild rivers and lakes. The hippopotamus, commonly known as the hippo, is an aquatic mammal known for its immense size, amphibious lifestyle, and unique role in the ecosystem. This chapter delves into the world of hippos, exploring their habits, characteristics, and the ecological niche they occupy.

Anatomy and Physical Characteristics
Hippos are the third-largest land mammal, after elephants and rhinos. Adult males can weigh up to 1,500 kg (3,300 lbs), while females are slightly smaller. Their barrel-shaped bodies, short legs, and almost hairless skin are perfectly adapted to an aquatic lifestyle. A hippo's eyes, ears, and nostrils are positioned on top of its head, allowing it to breathe and observe while mostly submerged.

Aquatic Adaptations
Hippos spend most of their time in water, which helps regulate their body temperature and supports their massive weight. Their dense skin secretes a natural sunscreen, often referred to as "blood sweat," which appears red or pink. This secretion is crucial for protecting their sensitive skin from sunburn and infection.

Behavior and Social Structure
Hippos are highly social and live in groups called pods, schools, or bloats, typically consisting of 10 to 30 individuals. These groups are usually dominated by a single bull. Within these pods, hippos display complex social behaviors, including vocal communications like grunts and wheezes, which are essential in maintaining the group's hierarchy and cohesion.

Feeding Habits
Contrary to their docile appearance, hippos are predominantly herbivorous, grazing on grasses at dusk. They can consume up to 40 kg (88 lbs) of grass each night. Their large mouths and sharp teeth are primarily used for defense and display, rather than for feeding.

The Hippo's Role in the Ecosystem
Hippos play a critical role in their aquatic ecosystems. Their grazing patterns help maintain the health of grasslands, and their movements in water create channels that improve water circulation and oxygenation. Hippo dung, deposited in rivers and lakes, is a key nutrient source for fish and other aquatic organisms.

Reproduction and Life Cycle
Female hippos reach sexual maturity at about five to six years and give birth to a single calf after an eight-month gestation period. Calves are born underwater and must swim to the surface to take their first breath. Mothers are fiercely protective, keeping their calves close for the first few years of life.

Threats and Conservation Challenges
Hippos face several threats, including habitat loss due to human encroachment and water pollution. They are also vulnerable to poaching for their meat and ivory-like teeth. In some regions, hippos and humans come into conflict, especially where agriculture encroaches on their habitats.

Conservation and Human Interaction
Efforts to conserve hippos include habitat protection, anti-poaching measures, and promoting coexistence with local communities. Understanding hippo behavior and ecology is crucial for developing effective conservation strategies.

The Cultural Significance of Hippos
In African cultures, hippos are often respected and feared due to their size, strength, and unpredictable nature. They are featured in folklore and art, symbolizing power, protection, and the mysteries of the water world.
Research and Monitoring
Ongoing research is essential for understanding hippos' behavior, population dynamics, and health. Monitoring their numbers and health helps in managing their populations and ensuring the stability of the ecosystems they inhabit.
The Hippo's Impact on Water Ecosystems
Hippos have a significant impact on the aquatic ecosystems of rivers and lakes. They help shape the physical environment and influence the biological diversity of these habitats, making their conservation essential for maintaining the ecological balance of Africa's waterways.

African Buffalo: The Formidable Bovines

The Quintessential Symbol of African Wilderness
In the diverse landscapes of Kenya and Tanzania, the African buffalo, a member of the Big Five, stands as a symbol of the untamed wild. Known for their formidable presence and unpredictable nature, these bovines are a keystone species in the African savanna. This chapter explores the life, behavior, and ecological significance of the African buffalo.

Physical Characteristics and Adaptations
The African buffalo, or Cape buffalo, is a large, robust animal with males weighing up to 900 kg (2000 lbs) and standing 1.7 meters (5.6 ft) at the shoulder. Both males and females possess horns; in males, these horns are characterized by a pronounced boss, a bony shield that fuses the horns at the base. Their dark brown or black coats and muscular build give them an imposing appearance.

Social Structure and Herd Behavior
Buffaloes are highly social animals, forming herds that can number in the hundreds. These herds are structured in a complex hierarchy that includes dominant males, females, and their offspring. Within the herd, buffaloes display strong bonds and are known to protect injured or sick members from predators.

Feeding Habits and Impact on the Ecosystem
African buffaloes are primarily grazers, feeding on a variety of grasses. Their grazing patterns play a crucial role in shaping the savanna ecosystem. By cropping the grass and stimulating new growth, they maintain the health of the grasslands and prevent bush encroachment.

Reproduction and Life Cycle
The breeding season of the African buffalo varies depending on the region, but it typically coincides with the rainy season when food is abundant. Females give birth to a single calf after a gestation period of about 11 months. Calves are born vulnerable but quickly gain strength and are able to stand and walk within minutes.

The Buffalo's Role in the Ecosystem
As a prey species for large predators like lions and hyenas, African buffaloes play a critical role in the predator-prey dynamics of the African savanna. They are also important seed dispersers, aiding in the distribution of plant species across their habitats.

Defensive Behavior and Predation
Despite being preyed upon by large predators, African buffaloes are known for their defensive capabilities. They are one of the few prey species that actively defend themselves and their herd members against predators. Their formidable horns and sheer strength make them a challenging target for even the most skilled predators.

Threats and Conservation Status
The main threats to African buffalo populations include habitat loss due to agricultural expansion, diseases like bovine tuberculosis, and poaching. In protected areas, they tend to thrive, but outside these zones, their numbers are often in decline.

Human-Buffalo Conflict
In areas where their habitat overlaps with human settlements, African buffaloes can come into conflict with farmers, especially when they raid crops. Mitigating these conflicts through community-based conservation strategies is essential for the coexistence of buffaloes and humans.

Conservation Efforts
Conservation efforts for African buffaloes focus on habitat protection and monitoring of diseases that can affect both buffalo and cattle populations. Anti-poaching measures and community engagement are also critical components of these conservation strategies.

The Buffalo in African Culture
In many African cultures, the buffalo is revered for its strength and resilience. It is often depicted in art and folklore, symbolizing strength, stability, and abundance.

Research and Monitoring
Ongoing research on African buffaloes includes studies on their behavior, social structure, and impact on ecosystems. Monitoring their populations and health is crucial for understanding their role in the ecosystem and for making informed conservation decisions.

The African Buffalo's Ecological Impact
The African buffalo's grazing habits, role as a prey species, and interactions with other species make it a vital component of the African savanna ecosystem. Their presence indicates a healthy, functioning environment, underscoring the importance of their conservation for the overall health and balance of the African wilderness.

Zebras: Patterns in the Plains

The Iconic Stripes of the Savannah
In the vast grasslands of Kenya and Tanzania, the zebra stands out with its striking black-and-white stripes, a distinctive pattern that has fascinated scientists and nature lovers alike. This chapter delves into the world of zebras, exploring their unique characteristics, social behavior, and the role they play in the savanna ecosystem.

Species and Physical Characteristics
There are three species of zebras: the Plains Zebra, the Mountain Zebra, and the Grevy's Zebra. The Plains Zebra, the most common species found in Kenya and Tanzania, is characterized by its broad stripes that run vertically on the neck and torso and horizontally on the hindquarters. Zebras are medium-sized equids, with adult males weighing up to 350 kg (770 lbs) and females slightly lighter.

The Mystery of the Stripes
The zebra's stripes have been a subject of scientific inquiry for years. Several theories exist regarding their purpose, with the most widely accepted being that the stripes may help deter biting flies, which are less likely to land on striped surfaces. Other theories suggest that the stripes aid in thermoregulation or serve as camouflage in the dappled light of the early morning and late evening.

Social Structure and Herd Behavior
Zebras are highly social animals, forming groups known as harems, consisting of one stallion, several mares, and their young. These harems often come together to form larger herds for added protection against predators. Stallions protect their harems with fierce determination, fending off rival males and predators.

Feeding and Grazing Patterns
Zebras are primarily grazers, feeding on a variety of grasses. Their digestive systems are well adapted to a high-fiber, low-nutrient diet, allowing them to thrive in habitats where other grazers might struggle. Zebras play a critical role in shaping the grasslands, with their grazing habits promoting new growth and maintaining the health of the savanna.

Predation and Defense Strategies
As prey animals, zebras are targeted by large predators such as lions, hyenas, and wild dogs. Their stripes may create a confusing visual effect known as motion dazzle when they move in groups, making it difficult for predators to single out an individual. Zebras also have a powerful kick, which they use effectively in defense.

Reproduction and Life Cycle
The breeding season for zebras varies depending on environmental conditions, but they can reproduce year-round. After a gestation period of about 12 to 13 months, a mare gives birth to a single foal. Foals can stand and run within an hour of birth, a crucial adaptation for survival in the predator-rich savanna.

Migration and Movement
Some populations of Plains Zebras participate in migrations, traveling hundreds of kilometers in search of fresh grazing and water. These migrations are among the most spectacular wildlife phenomena, with thousands of zebras moving alongside wildebeests and gazelles.

Conservation Status and Threats
Zebras face threats from habitat loss and fragmentation, competition with livestock, and poaching for their skins. Grevy's Zebra, in particular, is listed as endangered, primarily due to habitat loss and reduced access to water sources.

Human-Zebra Interactions
In areas where zebras come into contact with human settlements, they can conflict with farmers by grazing on crops. Efforts to mitigate these conflicts include community-based conservation initiatives and habitat management.

The Zebra in African Culture
In African cultures, zebras are often admired for their communal behavior and striking appearance. They appear in folklore and art, symbolizing harmony, balance, and social bonds.

Research and Monitoring
Ongoing research on zebras includes studies on their behavior, migration patterns, and social structures. Understanding these aspects is crucial for effective conservation strategies and ensuring the survival of these iconic animals of the African plains.

Zebras' Role in the Ecosystem
Zebras play an integral role in the savanna ecosystem. Their grazing habits influence the composition and health of grasslands, and as prey species, they are an essential link in the food chain. Their presence and behavior have a significant impact on the ecological dynamics of the plains, making their conservation vital for the health and diversity of the savanna.

The Baboon Troops: Societies in the Trees

Architects of Arboreal Communities
In the diverse ecosystems of Kenya and Tanzania, baboons are a common sight, their distinct presence a testament to the adaptability and social complexity of primates. This chapter delves into the intricate world of baboon troops, exploring their behavior, social structures, and the crucial role they play in their habitats.

Species and Characteristics
There are several species of baboons across Africa, but the most prevalent in Kenya and Tanzania are the Olive Baboon and the Yellow Baboon. These species are distinguished by their size, coloration, and range. Baboons are notable for their dog-like faces, powerful jaws, and long, muscular limbs that aid in both arboreal and terrestrial movement.

The Social Fabric of Baboon Troops
Baboon societies are highly complex and organized. Troops can consist of dozens to even hundreds of individuals. Within these troops, there are intricate social hierarchies maintained through grooming, mating, and various forms of communication. Males typically dominate the group, but female lineage also plays a significant role in troop dynamics.

Communication and Interaction
Baboons communicate through a range of vocalizations, body postures, and facial expressions. Their vocal repertoire includes barks, grunts, and screams, which convey different messages from alarm calls to social interactions. Grooming is not only a form of cleanliness but also a crucial social activity that strengthens bonds within the troop.

Feeding Habits and Foraging
Baboons are omnivorous, with a diet that includes fruits, seeds, leaves, insects, and small mammals. Their foraging behavior is a key aspect of their survival, as they can adapt their diet based on availability and season. This adaptability allows them to inhabit a variety of environments, from savannas to forests.

Reproduction and Rearing of Young
In baboon troops, mating is typically dominated by higher-ranking males, although females also exhibit mate choice. After a gestation period of around six months, females give birth to a single offspring. Baboon mothers are highly attentive, nurturing their young for several years. Young baboons learn social and survival skills within the troop, playing an important role in their development.

Predation and Defense Strategies
While baboons are preyed upon by large predators such as leopards and lions, they are adept at defending themselves. Their sheer numbers, combined with strong canine teeth and cooperative defense strategies, make them formidable opponents.

Habitat and Range
Baboons are among the most adaptable of primates, able to thrive in various environments. They are found in a range of habitats, from dense forests to arid regions. Their ability to live in close proximity to human settlements sometimes leads to conflict, particularly in areas where they raid crops.

Conservation and Human Interaction
Conservation efforts for baboons involve habitat preservation and managing human-baboon conflicts. As with many wildlife species, habitat loss and fragmentation are major concerns. Education and community engagement are crucial in fostering coexistence and mitigating conflict.

The Baboon in Research and Science
Baboons have been a subject of interest in primatological research due to their complex social structures and behaviors. Studies on baboon troops have provided insights into primate social dynamics, cognition, and evolution.

Baboons and Ecosystem Health
Baboons play a significant role in their ecosystems as seed dispersers and as a part of the food web. Their foraging habits impact the distribution and growth of plant species, while their role as prey influences predator populations.

The Baboon's Cultural Significance
In African cultures, baboons are often featured in folklore and mythology, symbolizing intelligence, trickery, and strength. Their presence in art and stories reflects their importance in the cultural landscape of Africa.

Monitoring and Conservation Strategies
Effective conservation of baboons involves monitoring their populations, understanding their interaction with ecosystems, and developing strategies to mitigate human-wildlife conflict. These efforts are crucial in ensuring the continued survival and health of baboon troops in the wild landscapes of Kenya and Tanzania.

Warthogs: Wonders of the Wild

The Endearing Residents of the Savannah
In the diverse terrain of Kenya and Tanzania, the warthog, with its distinctive appearance and quirky behavior, is a fascinating and often underrated inhabitant of the African wilderness. This chapter provides an in-depth look at the life and habits of warthogs, shedding light on their unique adaptations and important role in the ecosystem.
Physical Characteristics and Adaptations
Warthogs are members of the wild pig family and are easily recognizable by their large heads, protruding tusks, and the characteristic "warts" – thick protective pads on their faces. These animals are not particularly large, with adults typically weighing between 50 to 150 kilograms (110 to 330 pounds). Their coarse hair, sparse on their bodies but more prominent along the spine and tail, adds to their distinctive look.
Tusks and Warts: Tools for Survival
The tusks of warthogs, which are actually elongated canine teeth, are one of their most notable features. These tusks are not just for show; they serve as important tools for defense against predators and for digging up roots and tubers, which are staples of the warthog's diet. The warts serve a protective purpose, cushioning the face during fights.

Social Behavior and Lifestyle
Warthogs are social animals and are commonly found in family groups called sounders. These groups typically consist of a female and her offspring, although sometimes multiple adult females and their young band together. Male warthogs are more solitary or may form bachelor groups until they are old enough to compete for mates.

Diet and Foraging Habits
Warthogs are primarily grazers but exhibit a great deal of flexibility in their diet, which includes grass, roots, berries, and other plant matter. They are known for their habit of kneeling on their front knees while foraging, a unique adaptation among pigs that allows them to reach food close to the ground.

Reproduction and Raising Young
The mating season for warthogs generally coincides with the rainy season, when food is abundant. After a gestation period of about six months, the female gives birth to a litter of up to eight piglets, although two to four is more common. Warthogs use burrows, often taken over from other animals such as aardvarks, as nurseries for their young, providing protection from the elements and predators.

Survival Strategies and Predation
Despite their formidable appearance, warthogs are prey for many of Africa's large predators, including lions, leopards, cheetahs, hyenas, and crocodiles. Their primary defense mechanism is to flee, using their speed and agility to escape predators. When cornered, however, they can be fierce fighters, using their tusks effectively.

Habitat and Range
Warthogs are adaptable animals, found in a range of habitats from grasslands and savannas to woodlands. They require a water source for drinking and wallowing, which helps regulate their body temperature and remove parasites.

Human-Warthog Interactions
In areas where human settlements encroach on their natural habitat, warthogs can become a nuisance by raiding crops and gardens. However, they are also appreciated for their role in controlling certain pests and insects.

Conservation Status
While warthogs are not currently considered endangered, they face threats from habitat loss and hunting. In some areas, they are hunted for their meat and tusks, although in protected areas, they tend to thrive.

The Warthog in Culture
In African folklore and popular culture, warthogs are often portrayed as symbols of resourcefulness and survival. Their distinctive appearance and behaviors have made them a favorite subject in wildlife documentaries and films.

Research and Understanding
Ongoing research on warthogs helps in understanding their ecological role, behavior, and social structures. This knowledge is essential in developing conservation strategies and managing human-warthog interactions effectively.

Warthogs and Ecosystem Dynamics
Warthogs contribute to the biodiversity and health of their ecosystems through their foraging habits and as a prey species. Their interactions with the environment and other species highlight the interconnectedness of the African savanna and the importance of each species within this complex web of life.

The Dainty Dik-Dik: Tiny Titans

Unassuming Yet Resilient Inhabitants of the Bush
In the diverse landscapes of Kenya and Tanzania, amid the grandeur of larger mammals, resides a diminutive yet remarkable creature - the dik-dik. These tiny antelopes, often overlooked, are a testament to the intricacies and wonders of the African wilderness. This chapter is dedicated to exploring the lives, habits, and survival strategies of dik-diks in their natural habitat.

Physical Characteristics and Species Varieties
Dik-diks belong to the antelope family and are among the smallest of their kind. On average, they stand about 30-40 centimeters (12-16 inches) tall at the shoulder and weigh between 3 to 6 kilograms (6.6 to 13.2 pounds). There are four species of dik-diks, with the most common in Kenya and Tanzania being the Kirk's Dik-Dik. They are characterized by their elongated snouts, large, dark eyes, and the distinctive tuft of hair on their forehead. Males possess small, sharp horns that are often hidden in this tuft of hair.

Adaptations for Survival
Dik-diks have several adaptations that aid their survival in the arid and semi-arid regions they inhabit. Their elongated snouts help in cooling down their blood, a crucial adaptation for thermoregulation in hot climates. Their coloration, a blend of gray and brown, provides excellent camouflage against the bushveld.

Diet and Water Conservation
Dik-diks are browsers, feeding primarily on leaves, shoots, and fruits. Their diet is high in water content, which minimizes their need for drinking water. This ability to extract sufficient moisture from their food is vital for survival in habitats where water is scarce.

Behavior and Social Structure
Dik-diks are monogamous animals, forming lifelong bonds with their mates. They are territorial, with pairs marking and defending their territory against intruders. Their social structure revolves around these pair bonds, with minimal interaction outside of mating pairs and their offspring.

Reproduction and Offspring
After a gestation period of about six months, the female dik-dik gives birth to a single calf. Calves are well-developed at birth and can stand and walk shortly after. The mother hides her calf in the bush to protect it from predators, returning regularly to nurse.

Predation and Defense Mechanisms
Due to their small size, dik-diks are preyed upon by a variety of predators, including eagles, jackals, and leopards. Their primary defense mechanism is their ability to run in a zigzag pattern at speeds up to 42 km/h (26 mph), making it difficult for predators to catch them. They are also highly alert and rely on their keen sense of sight and hearing to detect danger.

Habitat and Range
Dik-diks are found in dry, bushy, and thorny habitats where they can easily hide from predators. They avoid open spaces and are rarely found far from cover. Their preference for dense brush and their small size make them less conspicuous in the wild.

Conservation and Environmental Impact
Dik-diks are not currently considered endangered, but they face threats from habitat loss and hunting. In some areas, they are hunted for their skins and meat. Their role in seed dispersal through their browsing habits makes them important contributors to their ecosystems.

The Dik-Dik in Culture and Folklore
In African folklore, dik-diks are often portrayed as symbols of diligence and vigilance. Their unassuming nature and strong pair bonds have made them a subject of admiration and interest in local cultures.

Research and Observation
Studying dik-diks provides insights into the survival strategies of small mammals in challenging environments. Research on their behavior, social structures, and ecological role contributes to a broader understanding of the dynamics of African ecosystems.

The Dik-Dik's Role in the Ecosystem
Despite their small size, dik-diks play a significant role in their ecosystems. As browsers, they contribute to the control of plant growth and the dispersal of seeds. Their presence indicates a healthy, balanced environment, underscoring the importance of small mammals in the biodiversity of the African savanna.

Flamingo Flocks: A Dance in Pink

The Vibrant Spectacle of the African Lakes
In the alkaline lakes of Kenya and Tanzania, the flamingo creates a mesmerizing display of color and grace. These iconic birds, known for their striking pink plumage and elegant posture, are a marvel of the avian world. This chapter is dedicated to exploring the fascinating world of flamingos, focusing on their unique characteristics, behaviors, and the ecological significance they hold in their habitats.

Species of Flamingos
The African region, particularly the Great Rift Valley lakes, is home to two species of flamingos: the Greater Flamingo and the Lesser Flamingo. The Greater Flamingo is the larger of the two, characterized by its lighter pink color and a black-tipped bill. The Lesser Flamingo is smaller, with more vibrant pink feathers and a deep red bill.

Physical Characteristics and Adaptations
Flamingos are known for their long, stilt-like legs and uniquely shaped beaks, which are specially adapted for their feeding habits. Their knees bend backward, and their ankles are located halfway up their legs. The beak is used to filter-feed on small organisms like algae, diatoms, and small crustaceans from the water.

The Pink Hue: A Dietary Tale

The flamingo's iconic pink color comes from the beta-carotene found in their diet. The pigments are metabolized and deposited in the feathers, legs, and beak. The intensity of the color varies with diet and species, with the Lesser Flamingo generally exhibiting a more vibrant hue due to its high intake of algae rich in carotenoids.

Social Behavior and Flocking

Flamingos are highly social birds, living in large flocks that can number in the thousands. These gatherings offer protection against predators and are essential for their breeding success. Their group behavior includes synchronized movements and displays, which are a captivating sight.

Breeding Habits and Colony Life

Flamingos breed in large colonies where thousands of birds nest closely together. They build their nests out of mud, creating cone-shaped mounds with a depression on top where the eggs are laid. Both parents take turns incubating the egg, and once hatched, flamingo chicks are fed a nutrient-rich milk produced by both parents.

Feeding and Foraging Techniques

Flamingos feed by stirring up the bottom of shallow waters with their feet and then scooping up the mud and water with their beaks. The beak's unique structure allows them to filter out food while expelling water and mud.

Migration and Movement Patterns

Flamingos are not migratory in the traditional sense but are known to move between habitats in response to changes in water levels and food availability. Their movements are often unpredictable, and they can travel long distances to find suitable feeding grounds.

Habitat and Environmental Importance

Flamingos primarily inhabit alkaline and saline lakes, wetlands, and lagoons. These habitats are crucial for their survival, providing the necessary food sources and breeding grounds. Flamingos play a vital role in these ecosystems, contributing to nutrient cycling and supporting biodiversity.

Threats and Conservation

Flamingos face threats from habitat loss, water pollution, and disturbance of breeding sites. Conservation efforts focus on protecting their habitats, monitoring populations, and researching their ecological needs and behaviors.

The Flamingo in Culture and Art

In many cultures, flamingos are admired for their beauty and have become symbols of grace and balance. They are a popular subject in art and photography, often representing the exotic and vibrant essence of the natural world.

Research and Monitoring Efforts
Ongoing research and monitoring are essential for understanding flamingo behavior, population dynamics, and migration patterns. This knowledge is crucial for effective conservation strategies and ensuring the long-term survival of these remarkable birds.

Flamingos and Ecosystem Health
The presence of flamingos is often an indicator of the health of wetland ecosystems. Their sensitivity to environmental changes makes them important sentinel species, signaling shifts in ecological balance. Protecting flamingos, therefore, contributes to the broader conservation of wetland habitats and the myriad of species they support.

The Ostrich: Sprinters of the Savannah

Majestic Giants of the African Plains

The ostrich, with its towering height and distinctive appearance, is a prominent figure in the savannahs of Kenya and Tanzania. As the world's largest bird, the ostrich is a symbol of the African wilderness, known for its remarkable speed and unique adaptations. This chapter delves into the fascinating world of the ostrich, exploring its biology, behavior, and the role it plays in its habitat.

Physical Characteristics and Adaptations

Ostriches are flightless birds, distinguished by their long necks, powerful legs, and large, round bodies. Adult males can reach heights of up to 2.8 meters (9 feet) and weigh between 100 to 160 kilograms (220 to 350 pounds), making them the heaviest and tallest birds on the planet. Females are slightly smaller and lighter in color than the males. Ostriches have two toes on each foot, with the main toe bearing a large, formidable claw. Their legs are incredibly strong and adapted for running, allowing them to reach speeds of up to 70 km/h (43 mph).

Feeding Habits and Diet
Ostriches are omnivores, consuming a variety of plant and animal matter. Their diet primarily consists of seeds, shrubs, grass, fruit, and flowers. They also eat insects, lizards, and other small creatures they find as they forage. An interesting aspect of their diet is their consumption of pebbles and small stones, which aid in grinding food in their gizzards.

Social Behavior and Group Dynamics
Ostriches are social birds, often found in groups that can range from a few birds to large flocks during certain times of the year. These groups are typically led by a dominant male and have a hierarchical structure. The social behavior of ostriches includes mutual preening, communal nesting, and complex mating rituals.

Breeding and Reproduction
The breeding season of ostriches is marked by elaborate courtship displays by males, which include bowing, wing flapping, and booming calls. Ostriches practice communal nesting, where a dominant female lays her eggs in a single large nest, which may also contain the eggs of other females in the group. Both males and females take turns incubating the eggs, which is unique among birds.

Egg and Chick Survival Strategies
Ostrich eggs are the largest of any bird species, each weighing around 1.4 kilograms (3 pounds). The eggs are incubated for about 40 days before hatching. Ostrich chicks are precocial, meaning they are relatively mature and mobile from the moment of hatching. The parents protect and care for the chicks, teaching them how to forage and survive in the wild.

Predation and Defense Mechanisms
Despite their size, ostriches are preyed upon by several predators, including lions, cheetahs, and hyenas. Their primary defense is their incredible running speed and agility. When threatened, they can also deliver powerful kicks capable of injuring or even killing a predator.

Habitat and Range
Ostriches inhabit a variety of environments, from open savannahs and grasslands to semi-arid regions and scrublands. They require open spaces where they can use their speed as a defense mechanism and have access to a variety of foods.

Conservation and Environmental Impact
Ostrich populations face threats from habitat loss, hunting, and predation. Conservation efforts focus on habitat protection and sustainable management practices, especially in areas where they are farmed for their meat, feathers, and leather.

The Ostrich in Culture and History
In African cultures and folklore, the ostrich is often revered for its strength, speed, and unique appearance. It has been a symbol of wealth and status in some societies and is featured in various cultural artifacts, stories, and dances.

Research and Observational Studies
Ongoing research on ostriches includes studies on their behavior, ecology, and physiology. Understanding these aspects is crucial for their conservation and for maintaining the ecological balance of their habitats.

Ostriches and Ecosystem Health
As part of the savannah ecosystem, ostriches contribute to seed dispersal and provide a source of prey for top predators. Their presence indicates a healthy, functioning environment, highlighting the importance of preserving these unique birds and their habitats.

Crocodiles: Stealthy Predators of the Waterways

The Silent Sentinels of Africa's Rivers and Lakes
Lurking beneath the surface of Kenya and Tanzania's rivers, lakes, and marshlands, the crocodile is one of Africa's most iconic and fearsome predators. Admired for their ancient lineage and feared for their predatory prowess, crocodiles are key players in the aquatic ecosystems of these regions. This chapter explores the life, behavior, and ecological role of crocodiles in their natural habitats.

Species of African Crocodiles
The most common species found in Kenya and Tanzania is the Nile Crocodile, one of the largest crocodile species globally. Capable of reaching lengths of over 5 meters (16 feet) and weighing as much as 750 kilograms (1,650 pounds), they are formidable creatures, with powerful jaws, sharp teeth, and a rugged, armored hide.

Physical Characteristics and Adaptations
Nile Crocodiles have a number of physical adaptations that make them efficient aquatic predators. Their streamlined bodies, webbed feet, and powerful tails enable swift movement in water. Their eyes, ears, and nostrils are located on top of their heads, allowing them to see, hear, and breathe while mostly submerged. They have a nictitating membrane that protects their eyes underwater and valves in their mouths that prevent water from entering their throats.

Diet and Hunting Strategies

Nile Crocodiles are apex predators and have a broad diet that includes fish, birds, mammals, and even other crocodiles. They employ a "sit-and-wait" hunting strategy, remaining motionless in the water for hours, waiting for an unsuspecting prey to come close. They then strike with lightning speed, seizing the prey with their powerful jaws.

Social Behavior and Territory

Crocodiles are territorial animals, particularly males, which can be aggressively protective of their stretch of river or lake. They exhibit a variety of behaviors for communicating dominance and submission within their social hierarchy. During the dry season, when water sources become scarce, crocodiles may congregate in large numbers in the remaining water bodies, creating a tense truce among normally solitary hunters.

Reproduction and Life Cycle

The breeding season of Nile Crocodiles typically occurs at the end of the dry season. Males attract females through a display of bellows and water dances. Females lay eggs in nests made of vegetation and mud, and guard them diligently. The temperature of the nest determines the sex of the hatchlings. Once the eggs hatch, the female helps carry the young to the water, showing a level of parental care that is unusual among reptiles.

Growth and Development

Crocodile hatchlings are vulnerable to a variety of predators, including birds, fish, and even other crocodiles. Juveniles grow rapidly for the first few years of life, feeding on insects and small aquatic animals. As they grow, they graduate to larger prey, eventually becoming apex predators in their adult years.

Threats and Conservation

While Nile Crocodiles are not currently endangered, they face threats from habitat loss and conflict with humans. In some regions, they are hunted for their skin, which is highly valued in the fashion industry. Conservation efforts include habitat protection, monitoring of populations, and programs to mitigate human-crocodile conflict.

Crocodiles in African Culture and Mythology

In many African cultures, crocodiles are respected and feared, often featuring in folklore and myths. They are symbols of strength, stealth, and survival, and are sometimes revered as sacred animals or seen as embodiments of deities.

Research and Ecological Understanding

Ongoing research on Nile Crocodiles includes studies on their behavior, physiology, and impact on ecosystems. Understanding these aspects is crucial for effective conservation strategies and for maintaining the ecological balance of Africa's waterways.

The Crocodile's Role in the Ecosystem

As top predators, crocodiles play a vital role in maintaining the health of aquatic ecosystems. They help control the population of certain fish and mammal species, and their predation helps to keep these ecosystems balanced. Their presence in a water body is often an indicator of the health and vitality of that ecosystem.

The Antelopes of Amboseli: Grace in Motion

Elegant Denizens of the African Plains
In the shadow of Mount Kilimanjaro, the Amboseli National Park in Kenya is a haven for a diverse array of antelopes, each species showcasing its own unique beauty and grace. This chapter offers a glimpse into the lives of these elegant creatures, their adaptations, behaviors, and the role they play in the Amboseli ecosystem.

Diversity of Species
Amboseli is home to several species of antelopes, each adapted to different aspects of the savanna environment. Prominent among them are the wildebeest, the gazelles (including the Thomson's and Grant's gazelles), the impala, the eland, and the lesser kudu. Each species possesses distinct features and behaviors that make them well-suited to their specific niches within the ecosystem.

Physical Characteristics and Adaptations
Antelopes in Amboseli are renowned for their agility and speed, crucial traits for evading predators. For instance, the Thomson's gazelle, one of the smallest but most common in the park, can reach speeds up to 80 km/h (50 mph). The impala, known for its elegant leaps, can jump up to 3 meters (10 feet) high and 10 meters (33 feet) in length. Elands, the largest of the African antelopes, have a more robust build and are notable for their spiral horns.

Social Behavior and Herd Dynamics
Antelopes exhibit varied social structures. Wildebeests and impalas tend to form large herds, which offer protection against predators. Gazelles may form smaller groups or even live solitarily, depending on food availability and predation pressure. The lesser kudu, being more elusive, is often found in small groups or pairs, staying close to dense bush cover for safety.

Feeding Habits and Ecological Role
Antelopes play a significant role in maintaining the balance of the savanna ecosystem. They are primarily grazers and browsers, feeding on a variety of grasses, leaves, and shrubs. This feeding behavior aids in seed dispersal and keeps vegetation in check, preventing overgrowth and promoting biodiversity.

Reproduction and Life Cycle
The breeding season for antelopes varies by species and is often influenced by the availability of food and water. Most antelopes have a gestation period ranging from six to nine months, after which a single calf is usually born. Newborns are precocial, being able to stand and run within a short time after birth, a critical adaptation for survival in predator-rich environments.

Predation and Survival Strategies
Antelopes are a key prey species for many of Amboseli's predators, including lions, cheetahs, leopards, and hyenas. Their survival strategies include keen senses of sight, smell, and hearing, vigilance, and living in groups where individuals can alert each other to danger.

Threats and Conservation Efforts
The antelopes of Amboseli face threats from habitat loss, human-wildlife conflict, and climate change. Conservation efforts in the park include habitat preservation, anti-poaching measures, and community-based initiatives to promote sustainable coexistence between humans and wildlife.

Antelopes in Local Culture
In the cultures of the communities surrounding Amboseli, antelopes are often revered for their beauty and grace. They feature in local folklore and are respected as integral components of the natural world.

Research and Monitoring
Ongoing research in Amboseli includes studying antelope behavior, population dynamics, and their role in the ecosystem. This research is crucial for developing effective management strategies for the park and for understanding the broader ecological dynamics of the East African savanna.

The Antelopes' Role in the Ecosystem
As herbivores, antelopes are vital for the health of the savanna ecosystem. They contribute to the control of plant growth, serve as prey for predators, and their migratory patterns help in nutrient distribution across the landscape. Their presence and well-being are indicators of the overall health of the ecosystem in Amboseli National Park.

Hyenas: The Misunderstood Scavengers

An Enigmatic Presence in the African Wilderness
In the savannas and woodlands of Kenya and Tanzania, the hyena is a ubiquitous presence, often shrouded in myth and misconception. This chapter seeks to demystify these intelligent and adaptable animals, highlighting their unique characteristics, social structure, and crucial role in the ecosystem.

Species of Hyenas
The African continent is home to several species of hyenas, but the most common in Kenya and Tanzania are the Spotted Hyena and the Striped Hyena. The Spotted Hyena, larger and more socially complex, is particularly prevalent in these regions.

Physical Characteristics
Spotted Hyenas are robust and bear a somewhat bear-like appearance. They have strong jaws, sharp teeth, and powerful neck muscles, adaptations that allow them to crush bones and access marrow – a nutrient-rich food source. Their coat is sandy, yellow, or brown, with dark spots that become fainter with age.

Social and Feeding Behaviors

Contrary to the common portrayal of hyenas as mere scavengers, they are efficient predators with a diet that includes a significant proportion of kills they make themselves. Their hunting strategy is based on endurance, often chasing their prey over long distances until it is exhausted.

The social structure of Spotted Hyenas is intriguingly complex and is often led by females, making them one of the few mammalian societies that are matriarchal. Clans can consist of up to 80 individuals, with a strict hierarchy that is maintained through various interactions and communications.

Communication and Intelligence

Hyenas communicate through an array of vocalizations, body postures, and facial expressions. The 'laugh' of the Spotted Hyena, often heard during social interactions, is one of the most distinctive sounds of the African bush. Studies have shown that hyenas are highly intelligent, with problem-solving abilities and social complexities that rival those of some primates.

Reproduction and Life Cycle

Female hyenas have a unique reproductive anatomy, with an elongated clitoris that closely resembles a male's penis, often leading to confusion regarding their gender. They give birth to one or two cubs, which are born with their eyes open and teeth erupted, ready to engage in the competitive environment of the clan.

Role in the Ecosystem

Hyenas play a crucial role in the African ecosystem as both predators and scavengers. By consuming carcasses, they help in nutrient recycling and in controlling the spread of diseases. As predators, they help maintain the balance of prey populations.

Conservation and Human-Hyena Conflict

Hyenas are often in conflict with humans, especially in areas where their natural prey is scarce, leading them to prey on livestock. This conflict sometimes results in hyenas being hunted or poisoned. Conservation efforts focus on mitigating these conflicts, understanding hyena behavior, and protecting their natural habitats.

Hyenas in Culture and Mythology

In African folklore and mythology, hyenas are often depicted in a negative light, associated with witchcraft and other superstitions. These cultural perceptions have influenced the way hyenas are regarded and treated in many societies.

Research and Understanding

Ongoing research efforts are crucial in understanding the complex social structures, behaviors, and ecological impact of hyenas. This research helps in dispelling myths and provides a clearer picture of these misunderstood animals, aiding in their conservation.

Hyenas and Ecosystem Health

As one of the top predators in their habitats, hyenas are important indicators of the health of the ecosystem. Their well-being reflects the overall health of the food chain and the environment they inhabit, making their conservation vital for the stability and diversity of African ecosystems.

The Vervet Monkey: A Prankster's Life

The Playful Inhabitants of the African Trees
In the diverse habitats of Kenya and Tanzania, from savannas to woodlands and coastal forests, the vervet monkey is a familiar sight. Known for their playful nature and intelligent behavior, vervet monkeys are a fascinating subject for those interested in the dynamics of primate life. This chapter delves into the world of vervet monkeys, exploring their characteristics, social structures, and the role they play in their ecosystems.

Physical Description and Species Varieties
Vervet monkeys belong to the genus Chlorocebus and are medium-sized primates. They have a distinctive appearance with silver-gray body fur, a black face, and a greenish tint on their backs. Adult males are larger than females, typically weighing between 4 to 8 kilograms (8.8 to 17.6 pounds), while females usually weigh about 3 to 5 kilograms (6.6 to 11 pounds). One of the most notable features of vervet monkeys is their bright blue scrotums, which are unique to the males.

Diet and Foraging Behavior

Vervet monkeys are omnivorous, feeding on a wide range of foods including fruits, leaves, flowers, and insects. They are opportunistic feeders and have been known to eat small birds and eggs. In areas adjacent to human habitation, they may also raid crops and steal food, which sometimes leads to conflicts with people.

Social Structure and Communication

Vervets live in highly social groups, usually consisting of 10 to 50 individuals. These groups are matriarchal, with females remaining in their natal groups for life and males leaving the group upon reaching adolescence. The social hierarchy is complex, with each monkey having a specific rank within the group.

Communication in vervet monkeys is sophisticated, involving a variety of vocalizations, facial expressions, and body postures. They have specific alarm calls for different predators, a trait that has been extensively studied and highlights their advanced cognitive abilities.

Reproduction and Maternal Care

Females reach sexual maturity around 2 to 3 years of age, while males mature around 4 to 5 years. The breeding season is dependent on the region and environmental conditions. After a gestation period of about 5 to 6 months, females give birth to a single infant. Maternal care is strong, with mothers being solely responsible for the care of their young.

Behavior and Play

Vervet monkeys are known for their playful and curious nature. Young vervets are particularly playful, engaging in games and mock fights, which help them develop social bonds and learn important survival skills. Their playfulness sometimes extends to teasing and stealing from each other, as well as from other species, including humans.

Adaptability and Habitat

Vervet monkeys are highly adaptable and can live in a variety of habitats. They are arboreal, spending most of their time in trees, but they are also comfortable on the ground. Their adaptability has allowed them to thrive in areas impacted by human activity, though this also puts them at risk of conflict with people.

Threats and Conservation

While vervet monkeys are not currently endangered, they face threats from habitat loss and hunting. In some regions, they are hunted for bushmeat and for traditional medicine. Conservation efforts focus on habitat protection and mitigating human-monkey conflicts.

Vervets in Culture and Science

In African folklore, vervet monkeys are often depicted as symbols of playfulness and intelligence. They have also been important in scientific research, particularly in studies of primate behavior and social dynamics.

Role in the Ecosystem

As omnivores, vervet monkeys play a role in seed dispersal and in controlling insect populations. Their foraging habits impact the vegetation structure and contribute to the biodiversity of their habitats.

Research and Observational Studies

Continued research on vervet monkeys is essential for understanding their complex social structures, communication, and interactions with their environment. This research contributes to our broader understanding of primates and aids in developing effective conservation strategies.

Mongoose: The Snakes' Nemesis

The Agile Hunters of the African Plains
The mongoose, a small yet fearless creature, is an intriguing presence in the ecosystems of Kenya and Tanzania. Famed for their snake-hunting prowess, mongooses are more than just simple predators; they are key players in maintaining ecological balance. This chapter explores the various aspects of mongoose life, from their unique physical characteristics to their complex social structures.

Physical Description and Species Diversity
There are several species of mongooses found across Africa, with the most common in Kenya and Tanzania being the banded mongoose, dwarf mongoose, and the larger white-tailed mongoose. Mongooses generally have a long, slender body, short legs, and a pointed snout. Their fur varies in color from gray to brown, and some species, like the banded mongoose, have distinct stripes or bands.

Diet and Hunting Behavior

Mongooses are primarily carnivorous, feeding on insects, crabs, earthworms, lizards, birds, and rodents. However, their diet can also include fruits and seeds. They are renowned for their ability to kill snakes, including venomous species. This is possible due to their agility, thick coat, and specialized acetylcholine receptors, which make them resistant, though not immune, to snake venom.

Social Structure and Group Dynamics

Many mongoose species, such as the banded mongoose, are highly social and live in groups called 'packs' or 'mobs'. These groups can consist of 20 to 40 individuals, exhibiting a complex social structure. Within these packs, mongooses cooperate in hunting, raising young, and defending territory. Dwarf mongooses are particularly known for their cooperative behavior, which includes sentinel duty, where one mongoose watches for predators while others forage.

Reproduction and Rearing of Offspring

Mongooses have a varied breeding strategy depending on the species. In many social species, breeding is synchronized within the group, leading to multiple females giving birth around the same time. This synchrony provides a survival advantage, as it reduces the risk of infanticide by males and allows communal rearing of the young.

Habitat and Adaptability

Mongooses inhabit a variety of habitats, from open savannas and grasslands to forests and marshlands. They are highly adaptable and can live in close proximity to human settlements. Their ability to thrive in diverse environments is attributed to their flexible diet and opportunistic hunting behavior.

Predation and Defense Mechanisms

While mongooses are predators, they are also prey for larger animals like birds of prey, snakes, and jackals. Their primary defense mechanisms include their agility, keen senses, and the ability to form tight-knit groups, which helps in detecting and deterring predators.

Role in the Ecosystem

Mongooses play a crucial role in their ecosystems. As predators, they help control populations of rodents and insects, thus impacting the ecological balance. Their hunting of snakes is also significant, as it controls snake populations and reduces the risk of snake-human conflict.

Threats and Conservation

Mongooses face various threats, including habitat loss, hunting for their fur, and persecution due to their occasional tendency to raid poultry. Conservation efforts for mongooses involve habitat protection and public education to reduce human-mongoose conflicts.

Mongooses in Culture and Folklore
In African folklore, mongooses are often portrayed as clever and resourceful characters. Their reputation as snake killers has given them a special place in the cultural fabric of the regions where they are found.

Research and Observational Studies
Ongoing research on mongooses includes studies on their social behavior, hunting strategies, and interactions with their environment. This research is crucial for a deeper understanding of their role in the ecosystem and for the development of effective conservation strategies.

Bushbabies: The Nocturnal Acrobats

Masters of the African Night
In the twilight hours of Kenya and Tanzania's forests and woodlands, the bushbabies, or galagos, emerge as enigmatic figures of the night. These small, nocturnal primates are known for their remarkable agility and haunting calls. This chapter explores the intriguing world of bushbabies, delving into their unique adaptations, behaviors, and roles in the African ecosystem.

Physical Characteristics and Species Diversity
Bushbabies are part of the family Galagidae and are characterized by their large, round eyes, which are essential for their nocturnal lifestyle. Their fur is typically soft and woolly, ranging in color from gray to brown. Bushbabies vary in size depending on the species, with some being as small as 10 centimeters (4 inches) in body length, not including the tail.

Adaptations for Nocturnal Life
The large eyes of bushbabies give them excellent night vision, crucial for spotting predators and prey in the dark. Their oversized ears are highly sensitive, able to detect the movements of insects and other small animals. Additionally, their strong hind limbs and long tails aid in their remarkable jumping ability, allowing them to leap several meters between trees.

Diet and Foraging Habits
Bushbabies are omnivorous, with a diet consisting mainly of fruits, tree gums, insects, and small animals. Their ability to vary their diet depending on availability makes them highly adaptable to different environments. They have a special tooth comb, used for grooming, and a long tongue, which is effective for lapping up tree sap and nectar.

Social Behavior and Communication
Bushbabies are generally solitary or live in small family groups. They are territorial animals and use vocalizations and scent markings to communicate and establish boundaries. Their calls vary from soft chirps to loud, eerie cries that can be heard at night, giving them the name "bushbabies."

Reproduction and Offspring Care
The mating system of bushbabies varies by species, with some being monogamous and others polygamous. Females typically give birth to one or two offspring after a gestation period of about four months. The young are born well-developed and with open eyes. Maternal care is intensive in the initial weeks, with mothers carrying their young and hiding them in nests or foliage when foraging.

Predation and Defense Mechanisms
Being small and active at night, bushbabies are preyed upon by a variety of nocturnal predators, including owls, snakes, and genets. Their primary defense mechanisms are their agility and leaping ability, allowing them to quickly escape danger. Their cryptic coloration also provides camouflage in the tree canopy.

Habitat and Range
Bushbabies inhabit a variety of forested and wooded habitats, including gallery forests, savanna woodlands, and coastal forests. They require trees with suitable foliage for cover and a source of gum, which is an important part of their diet.

Conservation Status and Threats
While some bushbaby species are abundant, others face threats from habitat destruction, hunting, and the pet trade. Conservation efforts for bushbabies include habitat preservation and legal protection against hunting and capture.

Bushbabies in Research and Folklore
Bushbabies have been subjects of fascination in African folklore, often associated with mystery due to their nocturnal habits and distinctive calls. Scientifically, they are studied for their unique adaptations to a nocturnal lifestyle and their role in forest ecosystems.

Role in the Ecosystem
As part of the forest and woodland ecosystems, bushbabies play a role in seed dispersal and pest control. Their foraging habits contribute to the pollination of some tree species and help regulate insect populations.

Research and Observational Studies
Research on bushbabies includes studies on their behavior, ecology, and physiology. Understanding these aspects is crucial for their conservation and for maintaining the ecological balance of their habitats. Their adaptability and resilience in changing environments make them an important subject for ecological studies in African woodlands and forests.

The African Wild Dog: Endangered Hunters

The Prowess and Plight of a Unique Canid
In the diverse wilderness of Kenya and Tanzania, the African wild dog (Lycaon pictus) is a symbol of the wild's untamed spirit. Known for their distinctive mottled fur, enduring stamina, and intricate social structures, these canids are among Africa's most efficient and cooperative hunters. This chapter delves into the world of the African wild dog, exploring their unique characteristics, behavior, and the challenges they face in their fight for survival.

Physical Characteristics and Identification
African wild dogs are medium-sized canids, with males slightly larger than females. They typically weigh between 20 to 30 kilograms (44 to 66 pounds). One of their most striking features is their irregularly patterned coat of yellow, black, and white, which is unique to each individual and aids in camouflage. They have large, rounded ears that provide excellent hearing and help in thermoregulation. Unlike other canids, wild dogs have only four toes per foot.

Social Structure and Pack Life
African wild dogs are highly social animals, living in packs typically consisting of 6 to 20 individuals, though larger packs of over 40 have been recorded. These packs are led by a dominant breeding pair. Their social structure is characterized by strong bonds, cooperation in hunting and pup rearing, and a unique hierarchy where aggression is uncommon, and submissive behaviors are more prevalent.

Hunting Tactics and Diet
Renowned for their endurance hunting technique, wild dogs can maintain a chase over long distances at speeds of up to 60 km/h (37 mph). They predominantly prey on medium-sized ungulates such as impalas, gazelles, and wildebeests. The pack works cooperatively to isolate and pursue their prey, with individuals taking turns in the chase. After a successful hunt, the kill is shared among all members, including the young and the sick.

Reproduction and Rearing of Pups
Breeding is typically monopolized by the dominant pair in the pack. After a gestation period of about 70 days, the female gives birth to a litter of 6 to 16 pups, one of the largest litter sizes in the canid family. The entire pack participates in the care of the pups, including regurgitating food for them and babysitting.

Communication and Vocalizations
African wild dogs communicate using a variety of vocalizations, body language, and scent markings. Their calls include high-pitched whines, huffs, and chattering sounds. These vocalizations play a crucial role in coordinating hunts and maintaining social cohesion within the pack.

Habitat and Range
Wild dogs are versatile in their habitat preferences but require large territories for hunting and denning. Their range includes savannahs, woodlands, and semi-desert regions. However, their habitat has been increasingly fragmented due to human activities.

Conservation Status and Threats
The African wild dog is classified as endangered, with only a few thousand individuals remaining in the wild. The major threats to their survival include habitat loss, human-wildlife conflict, disease (particularly canine distemper and rabies), and accidental killings in snares and road accidents.

Conservation Efforts and Challenges
Conservation efforts for African wild dogs include habitat protection, anti-poaching measures, and initiatives to mitigate human-wildlife conflict. Reintroduction and translocation projects have also been undertaken in some areas. A key challenge in wild dog conservation is their need for large territories, which often brings them into contact with human populations.

African Wild Dogs in Culture and Art
In African cultures, wild dogs are often admired for their cooperative and familial traits but have also faced persecution due to misconceptions and conflicts with livestock. In art and folklore, they are sometimes portrayed as symbols of unity and cooperation.

Research and Ecological Importance
Ongoing research on African wild dogs includes studies on their ecology, social dynamics, genetics, and interactions with other species. Understanding these aspects is crucial for their conservation and for maintaining the ecological balance of the regions they inhabit. As top predators, they play an essential role in controlling prey populations and maintaining the health of their ecosystems.

Servals: The Silent Stalkers

Elusive and Elegant Predators of the African Grasslands
In the vast expanses of Kenya and Tanzania's savannahs and wetlands, the serval, a medium-sized African cat, epitomizes stealth and efficiency in the wild. Known for their striking coat, exceptional hunting skills, and secretive nature, servals are among the most fascinating predators of the African ecosystem. This chapter delves into the world of servals, exploring their unique adaptations, behavior, and the challenges they face in their natural habitats.

Physical Characteristics and Adaptations
Servals are medium-sized cats, weighing between 9 to 18 kilograms (20 to 40 pounds), with males typically larger than females. They are characterized by their slender build, long legs, and a short tail. Their coat is golden-yellow with black spots and stripes, providing excellent camouflage in the tall grasses of their habitat. One of the serval's most distinctive features is their large, rounded ears, which sit atop a small head, giving them an incredible sense of hearing to detect prey.

Diet and Hunting Behavior
Servals are carnivorous, primarily hunting rodents, birds, frogs, insects, and fish. They have a unique hunting technique, using their long legs to leap high into the air and pounce down on unsuspecting prey, a strategy that is highly effective in the tall grasses of the savannah. They are also known to use their sensitive hearing to locate prey moving in the grass or underground.

Habitat and Range
Servals are found in a variety of habitats but prefer areas with tall grasses and abundant water sources, such as savannahs, marshes, and reed beds. They tend to avoid dense forests and arid deserts. Their range extends across much of sub-Saharan Africa, although their numbers are scattered and localized due to habitat fragmentation.

Social Structure and Territorial Behavior
Servals are solitary animals, coming together only for mating. They are highly territorial, marking their territory with urine and feces. The size of their territory varies depending on the availability of food and water but can be quite large to ensure adequate resources.

Reproduction and Life Cycle
The mating season for servals is not fixed and can occur at different times of the year. After a gestation period of about 74 days, the female gives birth to a litter of one to four kittens. The kittens are born blind and are cared for by the mother in a secluded den, usually in dense vegetation or abandoned burrows. They are weaned at about five months and become independent at around 12 months.

Threats and Conservation Status
While servals are not currently listed as endangered, they face threats from habitat loss, hunting for their skin, and persecution due to poultry predation. In some areas, their habitat has been significantly reduced due to agricultural expansion and human settlement.

Servals and Human Interaction
Servals are sometimes captured for the exotic pet trade, although they are wild animals and not suitable as pets. In rural areas, they can come into conflict with humans when they prey on poultry, leading to retaliatory killings.

Servals in African Culture
In African folklore and mythology, the serval is often admired for its beauty and grace. It is sometimes depicted as a symbol of vigilance and mystery, given its secretive nature and nocturnal habits.

Research and Monitoring
Ongoing research on servals includes studies on their ecology, behavior, and interactions with the changing landscape. Understanding these aspects is crucial for their conservation and for maintaining the ecological balance in their habitats.

Ecological Importance
As predators, servals play an important role in controlling the populations of rodents and other small animals, contributing to the ecological balance in their environments. Their presence in an ecosystem is often an indicator of a healthy, functioning environment.

Pangolins: Scaled Mysteries of the Night

Elusive Guardians of the African Wilderness
In the underbrush of Kenya and Tanzania's diverse habitats, the pangolin, a creature of enigma and grace, navigates the twilight world. These unique mammals, clad in a suit of protective scales, are among the most intriguing yet least understood of Africa's wildlife. This chapter delves deep into the life of pangolins, exploring their distinctive characteristics, nocturnal habits, and the conservation challenges they face.

Physical Description and Species
Pangolins, often called "scaly anteaters," belong to the order Pholidota. In Kenya and Tanzania, the most commonly found species is the Ground Pangolin. These remarkable creatures are characterized by their tough, overlapping scales made of keratin – the same material as human fingernails. Adult pangolins range in size, but most grow to about 65 to 80 centimeters (25 to 31 inches) in length, not including their long, prehensile tails.

Unique Adaptations for Survival
Pangolins are equipped with several unique adaptations. Their scales act as armor against predators; when threatened, a pangolin can roll into a near-impenetrable ball. They have long, sticky tongues, which can be extended to great lengths to collect ants and termites, their primary food source. Lacking teeth, pangolins grind their food with small stones and keratinous spines inside their stomachs.

Nocturnal and Solitary Lifestyle
Pangolins are solitary and predominantly nocturnal animals. They spend the daylight hours in burrows or hollows and become active at night to forage. Their solitary nature makes them elusive and difficult to study in the wild, contributing to the mystery surrounding these creatures.

Reproduction and Maternal Care
Pangolins have a slow reproductive rate. Females usually give birth to a single offspring after a gestation period of about five months. The young are born with soft scales, which harden within a few days. Mother pangolins are nurturing, carrying their young on their backs and protecting them in burrows.

Feeding Habits and Ecological Role
Pangolins feed primarily on ants and termites, using their keen sense of smell to locate nests. They play a critical ecological role in controlling insect populations, which helps maintain the balance in their habitats. Their foraging activities also aid in soil aeration and nutrient distribution.

Threats and Conservation Status
Pangolins are among the most trafficked mammals in the world. They face significant threats from illegal wildlife trade for their scales, which are falsely believed to have medicinal properties, and for their meat, considered a delicacy in some cultures. Habitat loss due to deforestation and agricultural expansion also poses a major threat to their survival.

Conservation Efforts
Efforts to protect pangolins include stricter enforcement of wildlife trafficking laws, habitat conservation, and public awareness campaigns to reduce demand for pangolin products. Research and monitoring are also critical for understanding their behavior and population dynamics, which are key to effective conservation strategies.

Pangolins in Culture and Folklore
In some African cultures, pangolins are revered and considered symbols of good luck and protection. They often feature in folklore and traditional stories, representing various virtues such as resilience and protection.

Research and Challenges
Studying pangolins is challenging due to their secretive and nocturnal nature. Research efforts focus on understanding their ecological needs, behaviors, and responses to environmental changes. This information is vital for developing effective conservation measures and ensuring the survival of these unique mammals.

The Pangolin's Importance in the Ecosystem
As insectivores, pangolins play an important role in controlling termite and ant populations, which can become pests if not kept in check. Their presence in an ecosystem is a key indicator of environmental health and biodiversity. Protecting pangolins, therefore, is not only about preserving a unique species but also about maintaining the integrity of the ecosystems they inhabit.

The Secretary Bird: Stalking the Savannah

A Unique Avian Predator of the African Plains
In the vast savannahs of Kenya and Tanzania, the Secretary Bird stands out as one of the most unique birds of prey. With its long legs, eagle-like body, and striking appearance, this bird is an unmistakable presence in the African grasslands. This chapter delves into the life and behavior of the Secretary Bird, exploring its hunting strategies, breeding habits, and the role it plays in the ecosystem.

Physical Characteristics and Distinctive Appearance
The Secretary Bird is a large, mostly terrestrial bird of prey, known scientifically as Sagittarius serpentarius. It stands about 1.3 meters (4 feet) tall, with a wingspan of up to 2.2 meters (7 feet). Its long, crane-like legs, short tail, and hooked beak make it unique among raptors. The bird gets its name from its crest of long feathers that resemble quill pens tucked behind an office secretary's ear.

Diet and Hunting Techniques
Secretary Birds are carnivorous and specialize in hunting terrestrial prey. Their diet primarily consists of insects, small mammals, and reptiles, including snakes. They are renowned for their ability to kill snakes, even venomous ones. Their hunting technique involves stalking prey on foot across the savannah and using powerful, rapid strikes with their feet to kill or stun their prey.

Habitat and Range
The Secretary Bird is found throughout the open grasslands and savannahs of sub-Saharan Africa. They prefer open areas where they can roam on foot, avoiding dense forests and very arid deserts. Their presence in a habitat is often an indicator of a healthy grassland ecosystem.

Social Behavior and Nesting
Secretary Birds are generally solitary or found in pairs. They are monogamous and known to form long-term pair bonds. Their nests are large structures built in the tops of acacia trees or on ledges of high cliffs. Both male and female participate in building the nest, incubating eggs, and feeding the young.

Breeding and Rearing of Chicks
The breeding season varies by region but often coincides with the dry season. The female typically lays two to three eggs, which are incubated for about 45 days. The chicks are altricial, meaning they are born relatively undeveloped and require care and feeding by the parents. Young Secretary Birds leave the nest at about 80 days but may remain with the parents for extended periods after fledging.

Threats and Conservation Status
The Secretary Bird is listed as vulnerable by the IUCN, with declining populations due to habitat loss, degradation of grasslands, and human disturbances. Other threats include pesticide use, which reduces their prey availability, and collisions with power lines.

Importance in Folklore and Culture
In many African cultures, the Secretary Bird is admired for its graceful appearance and its ability to control snake populations. It often appears in folklore and traditional stories as a symbol of strength and agility.

Ecological Role
As a predator, the Secretary Bird plays a crucial role in controlling populations of rodents, insects, and snakes. This not only helps in pest control but also maintains the balance in the ecosystem. Their presence contributes to the biodiversity and health of the savannah.

Research and Monitoring
Studying the Secretary Bird is important for understanding the health of savannah ecosystems. Research efforts focus on their breeding habits, hunting behavior, and movements across their range. Monitoring their population trends is crucial for conservation planning and for understanding the impacts of environmental changes on savannah habitats.

The Secretary Bird's Adaptation to Savannah Life
The Secretary Bird's adaptations for terrestrial hunting, including its long legs and ability to walk great distances, make it uniquely suited to the savannah environment. These adaptations highlight the evolutionary paths that different raptors have taken to exploit various ecological niches.

The Caracal: Elegance in Stealth

The Shadowy Predator of Africa's Wilderness
In the varied landscapes of Kenya and Tanzania, from savannas to scrublands and mountainous regions, lurks a predator marked by its elegance and stealth - the caracal. Known for its distinctive tufted ears and remarkable agility, the caracal is a testament to the adaptability and prowess of wild cats. This chapter delves into the world of the caracal, exploring its hunting techniques, physical characteristics, and the role it plays in its habitat.

Physical Description and Adaptations
The caracal (Caracal caracal) is a medium-sized wild cat, weighing between 12 to 18 kilograms (26 to 40 pounds) with males typically larger than females. It is characterized by a robust build, short coat, and distinctive long black tufts on the tips of its ears. The coat color varies from a reddish-tan to a pale gray, with white underparts. The caracal's strong hind legs and muscular build give it exceptional jumping ability, making it one of the most adept climbers and leapers among the small cats.

Diet and Hunting Behavior
Caracals are carnivorous, primarily hunting small to medium-sized mammals such as rodents, hares, and small antelopes. They are also known to prey on birds, reptiles, and occasionally livestock. Caracals employ a stealthy approach to hunting, using their acute senses and agility to stalk and pounce on their prey. Their ability to leap high into the air enables them to catch birds mid-flight.

Habitat and Range
Caracals inhabit a variety of environments but prefer areas with some cover for stealth and protection. They are adaptable and can be found in dry savannas, semi-deserts, scrublands, and mountainous regions. Despite being widespread across Africa, the caracal is rarely seen due to its secretive and nocturnal nature.

Social Behavior and Territoriality
Caracals are solitary animals, coming together only for mating purposes. They are territorial, marking their ranges with urine, feces, and scratch marks on trees. The size of their territory varies depending on the availability of prey and the density of the caracal population in the area.

Reproduction and Offspring
The breeding season of caracals is not strictly defined and can vary depending on the region. After a gestation period of about 78 to 81 days, the female gives birth to a litter of one to four kittens. The kittens are born blind and are cared for in a secluded den, usually among rocks or in dense vegetation. The mother solely raises the young, which become independent at around 9 to 10 months of age.

Threats and Conservation Status
Caracals are not currently listed as endangered, but they face threats from habitat loss, human-wildlife conflict, and hunting. In some regions, they are persecuted for preying on livestock. Conservation efforts for caracals include habitat protection, conflict mitigation strategies, and education to reduce persecution.

Caracals in Folklore and Culture
In various African cultures, the caracal is often admired for its beauty and hunting prowess. It has a certain mystique in folklore and is sometimes depicted as a symbol of cunning and agility.

Research and Ecological Importance
Research on caracals is important for understanding their role in the ecosystem as predators. By controlling populations of smaller mammals and birds, caracals help maintain the ecological balance. Their adaptability to different habitats makes them an important species for studying ecological resilience and biodiversity.

Caracals and Ecosystem Health
As a top predator in their environment, caracals are indicators of the health of their ecosystems. Their presence and population health reflect the overall wellbeing of the habitats they occupy, highlighting the importance of preserving these environments for a host of wildlife species.

The Honey Badger: Fierce and Fearless

An Emblem of Resilience in the African Wild
In the diverse and rugged landscapes of Kenya and Tanzania, the honey badger (Mellivora capensis) has earned a reputation as one of the most resilient and fearless animals. Known for its tenacity and remarkable adaptability, the honey badger navigates the African wilderness with an unparalleled boldness. This chapter explores the life, behavior, and survival strategies of the honey badger, a creature as enigmatic as it is formidable.

Physical Characteristics and Adaptations
The honey badger is a medium-sized mammal, with a distinctively robust and muscular build. They typically measure about 60 to 75 centimeters (24 to 30 inches) in length, with a tail adding another 20 to 30 centimeters (8 to 12 inches). One of their most notable features is their thick, tough skin, which is remarkably loose and allows them a significant range of movement within it. This adaptation is crucial for their defense, making it difficult for predators to maintain a grip on them.

Their fur is predominantly black, with a striking gray mantle that runs from the top of their head down their back. Honey badgers have strong, sharp claws used for digging and defending themselves.

Diet and Foraging Behavior

Honey badgers are omnivores with a varied diet that includes fruits, berries, roots, small mammals, birds, reptiles, and insects. They are particularly known for their fondness for honey and are adept at raiding beehives, a trait that gives them their name. Their foraging behavior is characterized by determination and resourcefulness, utilizing their strong claws and acute sense of smell to locate food.

Reputation and Behavior

Honey badgers have a well-deserved reputation for being fearless and aggressive when threatened. They are known to confront much larger predators, such as lions and hyenas, and are capable of inflicting serious injuries with their sharp teeth and claws. Despite their small size, their tenacity and ferocity make them one of the most respected and formidable animals in the African wild.

Habitat and Range

Honey badgers are found in a wide range of habitats, from dry savannas and scrublands to forests and mountainous regions. They are highly adaptable and can thrive in areas with diverse environmental conditions. Their ability to dig and climb allows them to exploit various microhabitats within these ecosystems.

Social Structure and Reproduction

Honey badgers are generally solitary animals, except during the mating season. Females give birth to one or two cubs after a gestation period of about six months. The young are born blind and rely entirely on the mother for the first few months. Mothers are known to be fiercely protective of their offspring.

Defense Mechanisms and Predation

Apart from their aggressive nature, honey badgers have other defense mechanisms. They have a gland at the base of their tail that secretes a pungent odor, used to mark territory and deter predators. Their thick skin and loose fur provide protection against bites and stings.

Threats and Conservation

While not currently considered endangered, honey badgers face threats from habitat loss, persecution due to their reputation as poultry raiders, and accidental poisoning. Their resilience and adaptability have helped them survive in changing environments, but conservation efforts are needed to ensure their continued existence in the wild.

Cultural Significance
In African cultures, the honey badger is often admired for its boldness and tenacity. It features in various folktales and is sometimes used as a symbol of courage and determination.

Research and Ecological Role
Studying honey badgers is important for understanding their role in the ecosystem. As predators and scavengers, they help control populations of rodents and other small animals, and their foraging habits contribute to seed dispersal and soil aeration.

The Honey Badger's Place in the Ecosystem
The presence of honey badgers in an ecosystem is an indicator of its health and diversity. Their role as both predator and scavenger makes them integral to the ecological balance, highlighting the importance of conserving these tenacious animals and their habitats.

The Bat-Eared Fox: Unseen Nighttime Forager

A Nocturnal Marvel of the African Plains
In the dim light of the African savannah, the bat-eared fox emerges as a unique and fascinating creature. With its oversized ears and nocturnal habits, it represents a distinct branch of the canid family tree. This chapter delves into the secretive world of the bat-eared fox, exploring its unique adaptations, diet, social behavior, and the important role it plays in the ecosystems of Kenya and Tanzania.

Physical Description and Adaptations
The bat-eared fox (Otocyon megalotis) is a small, African canid, known primarily for its large, bat-like ears, which can grow up to 14 centimeters (5.5 inches) in length. These oversized ears are not just for show; they are highly efficient at detecting insects and small prey, as well as helping to regulate body temperature. Bat-eared foxes have a gray to yellowish-brown coat, with lighter fur on their belly and dark markings on the legs, ears, and face. They weigh between 3 to 5 kilograms (6.6 to 11 pounds) and measure about 55 cm (22 inches) in length, excluding their bushy tail.

Diet and Foraging Behavior
Bat-eared foxes have a unique diet among canids, primarily consisting of insects, particularly termites and dung beetles. Their teeth are smaller and more numerous than those of other fox species, adapted for eating insects. They forage mainly at night, using their keen sense of hearing to locate prey. Their diet plays a crucial role in controlling insect populations and aids in soil aeration and nutrient recycling.

Social Structure and Mating Habits
Bat-eared foxes are social animals, typically living in small family groups consisting of a mated pair and their offspring. They exhibit monogamous behavior, with pairs often seen foraging and playing together. During the breeding season, males take an active role in caring for the young, which is somewhat unusual among wild canids.

Reproduction and Development of Young
The mating season for bat-eared foxes varies depending on the region but typically occurs during the rainy season when food is abundant. After a gestation period of about two months, the female gives birth to a litter of two to five pups. The pups are born blind and helpless and are cared for by both parents. They develop quickly, venturing out of the den to forage with their parents by the time they are a month old.

Habitat and Range
Bat-eared foxes inhabit the open savannahs and arid regions of eastern and southern Africa. They prefer areas with short grass and ample availability of their insect prey. Their presence in these habitats is an indicator of the health of the ecosystem, particularly the insect populations.

Threats and Conservation Status
While bat-eared foxes are not currently classified as endangered, they face threats from habitat loss due to agricultural expansion, predation by larger carnivores, and diseases such as rabies and canine distemper. Their reliance on specific environmental conditions makes them vulnerable to changes in their habitat.

The Bat-Eared Fox in African Culture
In African folklore and mythology, the bat-eared fox is often depicted with curiosity and intrigue due to its distinctive appearance and nocturnal habits. It is sometimes seen as a symbol of cleverness and resourcefulness.

Research and Ecological Significance
Research on bat-eared foxes is crucial for understanding their ecological role, particularly in controlling insect populations. They are important for the balance of their ecosystems, and studying their behavior and biology can provide insights into the health of the savannahs they inhabit.

The Bat-Eared Fox's Role in the Ecosystem

As insectivores, bat-eared foxes play a vital role in controlling pest populations, which can have significant impacts on the environment and agriculture. Their foraging habits contribute to the health of the soil and plant life, making them an important species for the sustainability of their habitats.

Colobus Monkeys: The Treetop Philosophers

Enigmatic Dwellers of the Canopy
High in the trees of Kenya and Tanzania's forests, the Colobus monkeys are a captivating sight. Their striking appearance and serene demeanor have earned them the title of 'Treetop Philosophers'. This chapter delves into the world of Colobus monkeys, exploring their unique characteristics, behavior, and the important role they play in the forest ecosystems.

Physical Description and Species
Colobus monkeys belong to the genus Colobus and are known for their distinct coloration and long, flowing tails. The most common species found in Kenya and Tanzania are the Black-and-White Colobus (Colobus guereza) and the Red Colobus (Piliocolobus tephrosceles). The Black-and-White Colobus is particularly striking, with its glossy black fur contrasted by long white mantle, whiskers, and tail tuft. Red Colobus monkeys are smaller, with a reddish-brown coat and a distinctive lack of thumbs.

Diet and Feeding Habits
Colobus monkeys are primarily folivorous, meaning their diet consists mostly of leaves, along with fruits, flowers, and twigs. They have a multi-chambered stomach, similar to that of ruminants, which allows them to digest tough and fibrous plant material efficiently. Their diet plays a crucial role in the forest's health by aiding in seed dispersal and maintaining vegetation diversity.

Social Structure and Group Dynamics
Colobus monkeys live in social groups, typically consisting of one dominant male, several females, and their offspring. The group size can vary but usually includes about 10 to 15 individuals. Social bonds within the group are strong, and members engage in grooming and other affiliative behaviors to maintain these bonds.

Communication and Behavior
Colobus monkeys communicate using a variety of vocalizations, body postures, and facial expressions. Their calls range from loud territorial choruses to soft contact calls within the group. These vocalizations are important for maintaining group cohesion and warding off predators or rival groups.

Reproduction and Maternal Care
Females give birth to a single infant after a gestation period of about six months. Newborns have a striking white fur, which gradually changes to the adult coloration as they mature. Mothers are the primary caregivers, although 'aunties' or other females in the group often assist in caring for the young.

Habitat and Range
Colobus monkeys are arboreal, spending most of their time in the treetops of both primary and secondary forests. They prefer areas with abundant foliage, which provides both their food and protection from predators. Their presence in a forest is often an indicator of a healthy, undisturbed ecosystem.

Threats and Conservation
Colobus monkeys face several threats, including habitat loss due to deforestation, hunting for their fur and meat, and the pet trade. Conservation efforts for these monkeys include habitat preservation, legal protection, and conservation education programs to raise awareness about their plight.

The Colobus Monkey in Culture and Mythology
In African cultures, Colobus monkeys are often revered for their beauty and are sometimes associated with mysticism due to their elusive nature and haunting calls. They are a symbol of the untouched, pristine wilderness.

Research and Ecological Importance
Research on Colobus monkeys provides valuable insights into primate ecology, social behavior, and forest conservation. As folivores, they play a significant role in forest dynamics, particularly in the dispersal of seeds and maintaining the diversity of tree species.

The Colobus Monkey's Role in the Ecosystem
Colobus monkeys are integral to the forest ecosystems where they reside. Their feeding habits aid in controlling the growth and spread of forest vegetation, and their role as prey supports a variety of predators. Their conservation is crucial for maintaining the balance and health of these forest environments.

Porcupines: The Prickly Wanderers

A Nighttime Forager of the African Bush
In the quiet of the African night, the rustling of leaves and the soft patter of feet herald the presence of one of the continent's most intriguing creatures: the porcupine. Known for their distinctive quills, porcupines are a symbol of self-defense and survival in the wild. This chapter explores the secretive world of porcupines in Kenya and Tanzania, their unique adaptations, behavior, and their ecological role.

Physical Description and Species Varieties
In Kenya and Tanzania, the most common species of porcupine is the Cape Porcupine (Hystrix africaeaustralis). These are among the largest rodents in the region, with adults typically weighing 12 to 20 kilograms (26 to 44 pounds). Their most distinctive feature is, of course, their quills. These are modified hairs made of keratin, stiff and sharp, used effectively for defense. The quills can vary in length, with some reaching up to 50 centimeters (20 inches).

Diet and Foraging Habits
Porcupines are primarily herbivores, feeding on a variety of vegetation, including roots, tubers, bark, and fruits. They have a strong preference for certain types of vegetation and can cause significant damage to crops and trees. Their powerful claws and keen sense of smell make them effective foragers, capable of digging up roots and bulbs with ease.

Social Behavior and Territoriality
Cape Porcupines are generally solitary or found in small family groups consisting of a mated pair and their offspring. They are territorial animals, marking their range with secretions from special glands located on their lower back. These areas are defended from other porcupines through displays of their quills and aggressive posturing.

Reproduction and Rearing of Young
The mating system of porcupines is monogamous, with pairs forming strong bonds. After a gestation period of around 94 days, the female gives birth to one to four offspring. The young are born relatively well-developed, with soft quills that harden within a few days. Parental care is shared by both parents, a rarity among rodents.

Quills as a Defense Mechanism
The quill defense system of porcupines is one of the most effective in the animal kingdom. When threatened, a porcupine will raise and spread its quills, making itself appear larger. If attacked, the quills can detach and embed themselves in the predator, causing injury. Contrary to popular belief, porcupines cannot shoot their quills; contact is required for the quills to detach.

Habitat and Range
Cape Porcupines inhabit a variety of environments, from forests and woodlands to grasslands and semi-arid regions. They prefer areas with ample food sources and cover for shelter. They are primarily nocturnal, spending the day in burrows or rock crevices.

Threats and Conservation
Porcupines face threats from habitat loss and hunting. In some areas, they are hunted for their meat and quills. However, they are not currently considered endangered. Their ability to adapt to different environments has helped them maintain stable populations.

The Porcupine in African Culture
In African folklore, porcupines are often depicted as symbols of defense and self-reliance. Their quills are sometimes used in traditional clothing and artifacts.

Ecological Role
Porcupines play an important role in their ecosystems. Their foraging habits aid in seed dispersal and soil aeration. As they dig for food, they help to cycle nutrients in the soil, promoting plant growth.

Research and Observation
Studying porcupines is important for understanding their impact on vegetation and their interactions with other species. Research on their foraging behavior, reproductive biology, and ecological role provides valuable insights into the ecosystems they inhabit.

The African Fish Eagle: Ruler of the Skies

A Majestic Emblem of African Waterways
Soaring high above the water bodies of Kenya and Tanzania, the African Fish Eagle (Haliaeetus vocifer) is a sight to behold. With its striking appearance and haunting call, it has become an emblem of African wilderness. This chapter explores the life, habits, and ecological significance of the African Fish Eagle, a bird revered for its prowess and beauty.

Physical Description and Identification
The African Fish Eagle is a large raptor, easily recognizable by its distinctive coloration. Adults have a brown body and wings, with a white head, neck, and tail. Their large, hooked beaks are yellow, as are their powerful talons. Males and females are similar in appearance, though females are generally larger. An adult can weigh between 2 to 3.6 kilograms (4.4 to 7.9 pounds) and have a wingspan of up to 2.4 meters (8 feet).

Diet and Hunting Techniques
True to its name, the African Fish Eagle primarily feeds on fish. It exhibits remarkable fishing skills; flying over water, it swoops down to snatch fish near the surface with its talons. Besides fish, its diet can include birds, small mammals, and even carrion. It is known to steal prey from other birds, exhibiting opportunistic feeding behavior.

Habitat and Range
African Fish Eagles are commonly found near freshwater lakes, rivers, reservoirs, and coastal lagoons. They prefer areas with abundant fish and suitable perching and nesting sites. Their presence near water bodies is a quintessential aspect of the African landscape and a signal of a healthy aquatic ecosystem.

Social Behavior and Mating
These eagles are monogamous and are known to form long-term pair bonds. Their courtship involves elaborate aerial displays, with loud calling and dramatic swooping movements. Couples often engage in duet calls, a synchronized calling that strengthens their bond and marks their territory.

Nesting and Reproduction
The nest of the African Fish Eagle, built by both members of the pair, is a large structure made of sticks and vegetation, usually located in a large tree or cliff ledge. Females lay 1 to 3 eggs, which are incubated primarily by the female while the male provides food. The chicks are altricial, requiring extensive care and feeding before they fledge.

Development and Lifespan
Chicks grow rapidly, developing flight feathers and learning to fly within about 70 to 75 days. However, they remain dependent on their parents for several months after fledging. African Fish Eagles can live for 12 to 24 years in the wild, depending on environmental conditions and predation pressures.

Vocalization and Communication
The call of the African Fish Eagle is one of the most recognizable sounds of the African wilderness. Their loud, distinctive cry, described as a ringing 'weee-ah hyo-hyo-hyo', is often used to proclaim territory and communicate between mates.

Threats and Conservation Status
While currently listed as Least Concern by the IUCN, African Fish Eagles face threats from habitat destruction, pollution of water bodies, and overfishing, which reduce their food sources. Conservation efforts focus on protecting aquatic ecosystems and ensuring sustainable fishing practices.

Cultural Significance
The African Fish Eagle holds a special place in many African cultures, symbolizing power, freedom, and majesty. It is featured in folklore, songs, and national emblems, representing the spirit of the African wilderness.

Ecological Importance
As a top predator in its ecosystem, the African Fish Eagle plays a crucial role in maintaining the balance of aquatic life. It helps control fish populations and, by feeding on carrion, aids in the ecosystem's nutrient cycle.

Research and Ecological Monitoring
Studying the African Fish Eagle provides valuable insights into the health of aquatic ecosystems. Research on their feeding habits, breeding patterns, and habitat preferences helps conservationists monitor ecosystem health and implement effective conservation strategies.

Aardvark: Oddities of the African Bush

A Nocturnal Marvel of Adaptation and Survival
In the mysterious nocturnal landscape of Kenya and Tanzania, the aardvark cuts a unique figure. This solitary, nocturnal mammal, whose name means "earth pig" in Afrikaans, is an extraordinary creature that has fascinated biologists and wildlife enthusiasts alike. This chapter provides an in-depth look into the life of the aardvark, exploring its unusual physical characteristics, behavioral patterns, and ecological role in the African bush.

Physical Description and Unique Features
The aardvark (Orycteropus afer) is a medium-sized, burrowing mammal, weighing between 40 to 65 kilograms (88 to 143 pounds). It possesses a peculiar appearance, with a long, pig-like snout used for sniffing out food, large, rabbit-like ears, and a kangaroo-shaped body with a thick tail. The aardvark's skin is tough and thick, providing protection from insect bites and harsh environmental elements. Its limbs are equipped with strong, curved claws designed for digging.

Diet and Foraging Habits
Aardvarks are specialized feeders, primarily consuming ants and termites. Their long, sticky tongue, which can extend up to 30 centimeters (12 inches), is perfectly adapted for lapping up these insects. They use their powerful claws to break into termite mounds or ant nests and can eat tens of thousands of insects in a single night. Their diet makes them important controllers of termite and ant populations in their ecosystems.

Nocturnal Lifestyle and Habitat
Aardvarks are nocturnal, spending the day in burrows and emerging at night to forage. They inhabit a range of environments, from dry savannas to rainforests, as long as there is an ample supply of ants and termites. Their burrowing habits play a crucial role in their survival, providing shelter from predators and extreme temperatures.

Social Behavior and Reproduction
Aardvarks are generally solitary animals, except during the mating season. Males and females come together briefly to mate, and then go their separate ways. Females give birth to a single calf after a gestation period of about seven months. The calf stays in the burrow for a couple of weeks before beginning to accompany its mother on foraging trips. Young aardvarks become independent at about six months of age.

Adaptations for Survival
In addition to their specialized diet, aardvarks have developed several adaptations for survival. Their keen sense of smell helps them locate food underground. When threatened, they can dig quickly to escape predators or retreat into their burrows, which they seal with soil.

Predation and Defense
Aardvarks are preyed upon by large African predators such as lions, leopards, and hyenas. Their primary defense is to flee and hide in their burrows. When cornered, an aardvark can use its powerful claws in defense, but its main survival strategy is avoidance.

Threats and Conservation
While not currently considered endangered, aardvarks face threats from habitat destruction and climate change, which affect their food supply. They are also sometimes hunted for their meat and are susceptible to diseases that can be transmitted from domestic animals.

The Aardvark in African Culture
In African folklore and mythology, the aardvark is often depicted with a sense of mystery and intrigue due to its nocturnal habits and unusual appearance. It is sometimes used as a symbol of resourcefulness and adaptability.

Research and Ecological Role
The study of aardvarks contributes to our understanding of biodiversity and ecosystem dynamics in African environments. Their role as insectivores makes them important for the control of termite and ant populations, impacting the balance of these ecosystems. Their burrowing behavior also aids in soil aeration and the creation of habitats for other animals.

The Aardvark's Place in the Ecosystem
The aardvark plays a significant role in its ecosystem, not only as a predator of insects but also as a prey species and a contributor to the ecological balance through its burrowing activities. Its presence is vital for the health and diversity of the African bush, making its conservation important for the stability of these environments.

The Bushpig: Kenya's Wild Swine

An Enigmatic Forager of the African Underbrush
In the dense forests and bushlands of Kenya, the bushpig (Potamochoerus larvatus) roams as a somewhat elusive yet integral part of the ecosystem. This wild swine species, often overlooked in favor of Africa's larger and more charismatic wildlife, possesses unique traits and behaviors that make it a fascinating subject of study. This chapter provides an in-depth exploration of the bushpig's lifestyle, habitat, and ecological impact.

Physical Description and Characteristics
Bushpigs are medium to large-sized wild pigs, with males typically larger than females. An adult bushpig can weigh between 55 to 150 kilograms (120 to 330 pounds). They are characterized by their coarse, bristly fur, which varies in color from reddish-brown to dark brown, and occasionally black. One of their distinctive features is the elongated snout, adapted for foraging, and the small, sharp tusks used for defense and digging.

Diet and Foraging Habits
Bushpigs are omnivorous, with a diet that includes roots, fruits, grasses, and a variety of animal matter such as insects, small mammals, and carrion. They are primarily nocturnal foragers, using their keen sense of smell to locate food. Bushpigs are known to cause damage to agricultural crops, leading to conflicts with farmers.

Social Structure and Group Dynamics
Bushpigs are social animals and typically live in small groups known as 'sounders.' These groups are usually composed of related females and their offspring, with adult males either solitary or forming smaller bachelor groups. The social structure within a sounder is relatively loose, but strong bonds are observed between mothers and their young.

Reproduction and Offspring
The breeding season for bushpigs is not strictly defined and can vary based on environmental conditions. Females give birth to litters of up to six young after a gestation period of about four months. The young are born in a well-hidden nest, constructed by the female from grass and leaves. The piglets are weaned at around three to four months but may stay with the mother for up to a year.

Habitat and Range
Bushpigs are adaptable animals found in a variety of habitats, including forested areas, riverine bush, and areas with dense underbrush. They are proficient diggers and often create burrows or use natural cavities for shelter during the day.

Threats and Conservation
While bushpigs are not currently listed as endangered, they face threats from habitat loss and hunting. In some regions, they are hunted for their meat and are considered a pest due to their crop-raiding habits. Conservation efforts for bushpigs are minimal, but they benefit indirectly from broader habitat protection initiatives.

The Bushpig in African Culture
In African folklore, the bushpig is often depicted as a cunning and resourceful animal. They are respected for their ability to survive in various environments and their tenacity.

Research and Ecological Role
Studying bushpigs provides insights into the functioning of forest and bushland ecosystems. As omnivores, they play a role in seed dispersal and soil turnover. Understanding their impact on vegetation and agricultural lands is important for developing effective management strategies in areas where humans and bushpigs coexist.

The Bushpig's Role in the Ecosystem
As part of the diverse wildlife of Kenya, bushpigs contribute to the ecological balance through their foraging habits and as prey for larger predators. Their presence in an ecosystem indicates a healthy, functioning environment, highlighting the importance of conserving these often-overlooked animals.

The Martial Eagle: The Aerial Predator

Majesty and Might in the African Skies
The Martial Eagle (Polemaetus bellicosus), a symbol of power and precision, reigns supreme in the skies of Kenya and Tanzania. As one of Africa's largest and most formidable birds of prey, it commands awe and respect. This chapter delves into the life of the Martial Eagle, exploring its hunting prowess, unique characteristics, and the vital role it plays in the ecosystem.

Physical Description and Identification
The Martial Eagle is a massive raptor, with a wingspan reaching up to 2.6 meters (8.5 feet) and weighing between 3 to 6.2 kilograms (6.6 to 13.7 pounds), with females generally larger than males. It is characterized by its dark brown plumage with lighter, speckled underparts and a distinctive white belly. The head and neck are pale grey, and the eyes are a striking yellow. Juvenile Martial Eagles are more mottled with brown and white and develop the adult plumage over several years.

Diet and Hunting Techniques
As top predators, Martial Eagles have a varied diet that includes birds, reptiles, and mammals. They are known to take down prey as large as monkeys, small antelopes, and large birds like storks or guineafowl. Their hunting strategy involves soaring at great heights, using their keen eyesight to spot potential prey before making a swift, powerful dive to capture it. They are also known to hunt by perching in a tree and ambushing prey.

Habitat and Range
Martial Eagles are found across sub-Saharan Africa, favoring open habitats such as savannahs, semi-deserts, and open woodland. They require large territories for hunting, often covering areas of over 100 square kilometers (39 square miles). These eagles are typically solitary, only coming together during mating season.

Breeding and Nesting Habits
Martial Eagles are monogamous, with pairs forming long-lasting bonds. They build large nests in the forks of tall trees, often returning to the same nest year after year. The female lays a single egg, which is incubated for about 45 to 53 days, primarily by the female while the male provides food. The chick is dependent on the parents for up to eight months, a relatively long parental care period among birds.

Threats and Conservation Status
The Martial Eagle is classified as Vulnerable by the IUCN, with populations declining due to habitat loss, persecution, and poisoning. These eagles are often targeted by farmers due to their perceived threat to livestock, despite their important ecological role.

The Martial Eagle in African Culture
In many African cultures, the Martial Eagle is admired for its strength and is often seen as a symbol of freedom and power. Its image is used in folklore and as a totem in various communities.

Research and Ecological Importance
Studying the Martial Eagle is vital for understanding the health of the ecosystems in which they live. As apex predators, their presence indicates a balanced ecosystem. They play a critical role in controlling populations of medium-sized mammals and birds, maintaining the ecological equilibrium.

The Martial Eagle's Adaptations
The Martial Eagle's adaptations for hunting, including its incredible eyesight, powerful talons, and exceptional flying ability, make it one of the most efficient predators in the African skies. These adaptations highlight the evolutionary success of this species in the diverse African landscape.

Conservation Efforts
Conservation efforts for the Martial Eagle include habitat protection, research into their ecology and breeding habits, and initiatives to reduce human-eagle conflicts. Public education campaigns are also crucial in changing perceptions and reducing threats from human activities.

Pelicans of the Rift Valley: Masters of the Water

Elegant Waterbirds of East Africa
Gracing the lakes of the Great Rift Valley in Kenya and Tanzania, pelicans are some of the most recognizable and majestic waterbirds. These large birds are admired for their impressive size, graceful flight, and unique fishing techniques. This chapter explores the world of Rift Valley pelicans, focusing on their biology, behavior, and the vital role they play in the aquatic ecosystems.

Physical Description and Species
The Rift Valley is primarily home to two species of pelicans: the Pink-backed Pelican (Pelecanus rufescens) and the Great White Pelican (Pelecanus onocrotalus). Both species are large and stocky with long bills and a distinctive throat pouch used for catching fish. The Great White Pelican is one of the world's largest flying birds, with a wingspan that can exceed 3 meters (10 feet). The Pink-backed Pelican is smaller, with a wingspan of around 2.5 meters (8 feet). Both species are predominantly white, but the Pink-backed Pelican has a pinkish hue on its back, as its name suggests.

Diet and Feeding Habits
Pelicans are primarily piscivorous, feeding mostly on fish. They have a unique and cooperative way of fishing, where groups of pelicans will work together to herd fish into shallow waters before scooping them up in their large bills. This method of group foraging is not only efficient but also a remarkable example of their social behavior.

Habitat and Adaptation
Pelicans in the Rift Valley inhabit freshwater lakes, swamps, and marshes. They are well-adapted to life in and around water. Their webbed feet make them powerful swimmers, and their large wings allow for efficient soaring flight, which is often used to travel long distances between feeding and nesting sites.

Social Behavior and Breeding
Pelicans are social birds, often seen in large flocks. They breed in colonies, which can number in the hundreds or even thousands of individuals. Nesting sites are typically located on islands or secluded shores, safe from predators. Both parents take part in incubating the eggs and feeding the young. The breeding season is synchronized with the availability of food, which ensures ample resources for raising their chicks.

Reproduction and Life Cycle
Pelicans lay two to three eggs, and the incubation period lasts about 30 to 36 days. The chicks are born blind and naked but grow quickly, fed by regurgitated fish from both parents. Fledging occurs around 3 months of age, but the young may stay with their parents for several more weeks before becoming fully independent.

Threats and Conservation
Pelicans in the Rift Valley face several threats, including habitat loss, water pollution, and disturbance of breeding colonies by humans. Fluctuations in water levels due to climatic changes also affect their breeding and feeding grounds. Conservation efforts for pelicans include protecting their habitats, monitoring populations, and regulating fishing practices to ensure sustainable fish populations.

The Pelican in Culture and Mythology
In the cultures around the Rift Valley, pelicans are often admired for their communal living and cooperative fishing techniques. They are symbols of abundance and teamwork in local folklore.

Ecological Role and Importance
As predators at the top of the aquatic food chain, pelicans play a crucial role in maintaining the balance of fish populations in the Rift Valley's lakes. Their presence is an indicator of the health of aquatic ecosystems. Studying pelicans also provides valuable insights into the impacts of environmental changes on these ecosystems.

Research and Monitoring
Ongoing research on pelicans in the Rift Valley includes studies on their migratory patterns, breeding success, and feeding behavior. This research is essential for understanding their ecological needs and implementing effective conservation strategies to protect these magnificent birds and their habitats.

The African Python: Silent Giant of the Savannah

A Formidable Predator in the African Wilderness
Lurking in the grasslands, swamps, and forests of Kenya and Tanzania, the African Python, specifically the African Rock Python (Python sebae), is one of the continent's most impressive reptiles. This chapter delves into the fascinating world of the African Python, exploring its physical attributes, behavior, and the vital role it plays in the ecosystem.

Physical Description and Characteristics
The African Rock Python is one of the largest species of snakes in the world. Adult pythons can reach lengths of up to 6 meters (20 feet), although specimens exceeding 4.5 meters (15 feet) are rare. They have a robust body with a distinctively patterned skin, featuring a series of irregular dark brown blotches bordered by a lighter color, against a background of olive, brown, or grey. Their skin pattern provides excellent camouflage in their natural habitat.

Diet and Hunting Strategy
African Pythons are non-venomous constrictors and formidable predators. They primarily feed on a diverse range of animals, including rodents, birds, monkeys, antelopes, and even crocodiles. Their hunting strategy involves ambushing prey, striking rapidly, and then coiling around it. They constrict their prey until asphyxiation occurs, after which they consume it whole.

Habitat and Distribution
These pythons are adaptable and can thrive in various habitats, including savannas, rainforests, swamps, and near water bodies. They often reside in abandoned animal burrows, dense vegetation, or rocky outcrops. Their choice of habitat is generally influenced by the availability of prey and suitable shelter.

Behavior and Lifestyle
African Pythons are primarily nocturnal, especially when hunting. They are solitary creatures, coming together only during the mating season. They are known for their ability to swim and can be found basking in the sun near water bodies during the day. Despite their formidable size, they are generally shy and will avoid human contact whenever possible.

Reproduction and Offspring
The mating season for African Pythons occurs during the dry season. Females lay clutches of 20 to 100 eggs, which they incubate by coiling around them and generating heat through muscle contractions. This maternal care is unusual among snakes. The hatchlings are independent from birth and receive no further care from the mother.

Threats and Conservation Status
The African Rock Python faces threats from habitat loss, hunting for their skin, and persecution due to fear. They are often killed on sight by humans. While they are not currently listed as endangered, their populations are under pressure in some areas. Conservation efforts are focused on habitat protection and raising public awareness to reduce fear and misunderstanding.

The African Python in Culture and Mythology
In many African cultures, pythons are revered and often associated with strength, mystery, and spiritual significance. They are featured in folklore and traditional rituals in various communities across the continent.

Ecological Role
As apex predators, African Pythons play a crucial role in controlling the populations of their prey, thus maintaining the balance of the ecosystems they inhabit. Their presence is indicative of a healthy, functioning environment.

Research and Ecological Importance
Studying the African Python provides valuable insights into the health of ecosystems in Kenya and Tanzania. Research on their diet, habitat preferences, and breeding habits helps in understanding the dynamics of these ecosystems and the impact of environmental changes. Conservation of the African Python is essential not only for the species itself but also for the biodiversity of the regions they inhabit.

The Nile Monitor: River Sentinel

A Reptilian Behemoth of Africa's Waterways
Along the banks of rivers, lakes, and swamps in Kenya and Tanzania, the Nile Monitor (Varanus niloticus) reigns as a formidable presence. This large lizard, known for its powerful build and aquatic prowess, is a fascinating subject of ecological importance. This chapter explores the intriguing world of the Nile Monitor, shedding light on its lifestyle, behavior, and the ecological niche it occupies.

Physical Description and Adaptations
The Nile Monitor is one of Africa's largest lizards, with adults commonly reaching lengths of up to 2 meters (6.5 feet), including the tail. They have muscular bodies, strong legs, and sharp claws adapted for climbing, digging, and swimming. Their skin is tough and rough, with a pattern of light and dark bands on the body and tail, providing excellent camouflage among the vegetation and muddy banks of their habitats.

Diet and Foraging Habits
Nile Monitors are carnivorous and have a diverse diet that includes fish, frogs, smaller reptiles, birds, insects, and carrion. They are opportunistic feeders, also known to raid crocodile nests to feed on eggs. Their acute sense of smell helps them locate food, and they are adept at both swimming and climbing trees in pursuit of prey.

Habitat and Range
These monitors are highly adaptable and can be found in a range of aquatic environments, including rivers, lakes, and wetlands. They are comfortable both in water and on land, often seen basking on riverbanks or in trees near water bodies. Their ability to thrive in various habitats contributes to their widespread distribution in sub-Saharan Africa.

Behavior and Lifestyle

Nile Monitors are solitary and territorial reptiles. They are known for their aggressive demeanor, especially when cornered or threatened. These monitors are excellent swimmers, using their long, laterally compressed tails to propel themselves through water. On land, they can run quickly and are skilled climbers.

Reproduction and Nesting

The breeding season of the Nile Monitor varies depending on the climate and region. Females lay clutches of up to 60 eggs, often using termite mounds or sandy banks as nesting sites. The heat generated by the termite mounds helps incubate the eggs. Hatchlings are independent from birth and quickly adapt to a life of foraging and surviving on their own.

Threats and Conservation Status

While the Nile Monitor is not currently considered endangered, it faces threats from habitat destruction and hunting. In some regions, they are hunted for their skin and meat. Additionally, their predation on poultry and eggs sometimes leads to conflicts with humans.

The Nile Monitor in African Culture

In many African communities, the Nile Monitor is respected for its strength and survival skills. It features in various local myths and folklore, often symbolizing adaptability and resourcefulness.

Ecological Role

Nile Monitors play a significant role in their ecosystems. As predators, they help control the populations of various aquatic and terrestrial species. Their scavenging habits also make them important for the nutrient cycle within their environments.

Research and Monitoring

Studying Nile Monitors provides insights into the health of aquatic ecosystems. Research on their population dynamics, diet, and habitat preferences is crucial for understanding the balance of the ecosystems they inhabit and for informing conservation strategies.

The Nile Monitor's Place in the Ecosystem

The presence of the Nile Monitor in an ecosystem indicates a healthy, functioning aquatic environment. They are an important part of the biodiversity in African waterways, contributing to the ecological complexity of these habitats. Conservation of the Nile Monitor is essential for maintaining the ecological integrity of rivers, lakes, and wetlands in Kenya and Tanzania.

Jackals: The Opportunistic Omnivores

Cunning Survivors of the African Savannah
In the diverse ecosystems of Kenya and Tanzania, jackals are a common yet captivating sight. These small, opportunistic omnivores, known for their adaptability and resourcefulness, play a critical role in the balance of their habitats. This chapter delves into the world of jackals, examining their physical characteristics, behavior, and the important role they play in the African savannah.

Physical Description and Species Varieties
There are three species of jackals commonly found in Kenya and Tanzania: the Black-backed Jackal (Canis mesomelas), the Side-striped Jackal (Canis adustus), and the Golden Jackal (Canis aureus). Each species has distinct physical features. The Black-backed Jackal is recognized by its silver-black fur with a reddish-brown flank and legs, the Side-striped Jackal by its muted brown coat with a prominent white stripe along the sides, and the Golden Jackal by its golden-colored coat. Adult jackals weigh between 6 to 15 kilograms (13 to 33 pounds), with males generally being larger than females.

Diet and Feeding Habits
Jackals are omnivorous and display great flexibility in their diet. Their diet includes a variety of foods, such as small mammals, birds, insects, fruits, and carrion. They are known to scavenge leftovers from larger predators' kills, but they are also efficient hunters in their own right, capable of catching small, fast-moving prey.

Habitat and Adaptation
Jackals inhabit a range of environments, including savannas, deserts, marshes, and mountains. Their adaptability to different habitats is one of their most remarkable traits. They are capable of surviving in both arid and lush environments, adjusting their diet and behavior according to the available resources.

Social Behavior and Group Dynamics
Jackals typically live in monogamous pairs, which may be accompanied by their offspring from previous seasons. They are territorial animals, marking and defending their territories from other jackals. Communication within and between jackal families is complex and includes a range of vocalizations, scent markings, and body language.

Reproduction and Rearing of Young
Jackal pairs are generally monogamous, with strong pair bonds. The breeding season varies depending on the species and the environmental conditions. After a gestation period of about 60 days, the female gives birth to a litter of 2 to 7 pups. Both parents participate in the rearing of the pups, which includes feeding, grooming, and teaching them hunting skills.

Predation and Defense Strategies
While jackals are predators, they are also prey for larger carnivores like lions and hyenas. Their primary defense mechanisms include their agility, cunning, and ability to stay hidden. They are also known for their loud and aggressive calls when threatened, which can alert other jackals in the area or deter smaller predators.

Threats and Conservation
Jackals face various threats, including habitat loss, persecution due to their reputation as livestock predators, and diseases like rabies and canine distemper. Despite these challenges, jackals are not currently considered endangered due to their adaptability and high reproductive rates.

The Jackal in African Culture
In African folklore, jackals are often portrayed as clever and cunning creatures. They appear in numerous stories and myths, sometimes as symbols of wisdom, and other times as tricksters.

Ecological Role
Jackals play an important role in their ecosystems. As omnivores, they help control rodent populations and clean up carrion, thus contributing to the health of their habitats. Their scavenging habits also aid in nutrient recycling within the ecosystem.

Research and Ecological Significance
Studying jackals provides valuable insights into the functioning of savannah ecosystems. Their behavior, diet, and social structures offer important clues about the health of their habitats and the impact of environmental changes on smaller carnivore populations.

The Ground Hornbill: The Ground-Dwelling Avian

A Unique Bird of the African Savannah
In the sprawling landscapes of Kenya and Tanzania, the Ground Hornbill is a distinctive and charismatic bird, known for its unique ground-dwelling habits and striking appearance. This large, terrestrial bird belongs to the family Bucorvidae and is notable for its size, coloration, and behavior. This chapter delves into the fascinating world of the Ground Hornbill, exploring its physical characteristics, lifestyle, and the role it plays in its ecosystem.

Physical Description and Species
The most commonly found species in East Africa is the Southern Ground Hornbill (Bucorvus leadbeateri). It is a large bird, standing up to a meter in height and weighing between 4 to 6 kilograms (8.8 to 13.2 pounds). The bird is predominantly black with vivid red patches of bare skin on the face and throat, which are more prominent in males. The beak is long, curved, and powerful. One of the bird's striking features is its long eyelashes, which are unusual for bird species.

Diet and Foraging Behavior
Ground Hornbills are omnivorous, with a diet that includes insects, reptiles, small mammals, and birds. They are also known to consume fruits and seeds. Their foraging behavior is distinctive; they walk through grasslands and savannas, using their strong bills to probe and dig for food. They are effective at controlling populations of potentially harmful insects and small animals.

Habitat and Adaptation
These birds are adapted to a variety of habitats, including savannas, woodlands, and grasslands. They require large territories for foraging, and areas with tall trees are preferred for nesting and roosting. Their adaptation to ground living is unique among hornbills, as most other species are arboreal.

Social Behavior and Group Dynamics
Ground Hornbills live in social groups typically comprising 2 to 12 individuals. These groups are often family units consisting of a breeding pair and their offspring from various years. The species exhibits cooperative breeding behavior, where older offspring assist their parents in raising the young.

Reproduction and Nesting
The breeding process of Ground Hornbills is slow and meticulous. They typically use large cavities in trees for nesting, and the female lays 1 to 2 eggs. The female incubates the eggs while being sealed inside the nest cavity by the male, leaving a small slit through which he feeds her and, later, the chicks. Only one chick usually survives as it receives the majority of the care and food.

Threats and Conservation Status
The Southern Ground Hornbill is classified as Vulnerable by the IUCN. The primary threats to this species are habitat loss, reduction in prey due to pesticide use, and direct persecution. Their low reproductive rate and the loss of suitable nesting sites contribute to their declining numbers.

The Ground Hornbill in African Culture
In many African cultures, Ground Hornbills are regarded with reverence and are often featured in folklore and traditional stories. They are sometimes associated with rainmaking and other supernatural phenomena.

Ecological Role
As predators and scavengers, Ground Hornbills play an important role in controlling populations of various ground-dwelling creatures. They are also seed dispersers, contributing to the health and diversity of their habitats.

Research and Monitoring
Research on Ground Hornbills is crucial for understanding their ecological requirements and social structure. Conservation efforts include habitat protection, breeding programs, and initiatives to restore their numbers in the wild. Their unique behaviors and role in the ecosystem make them an important species for ecological study in the savannas and woodlands of Africa.

The African Civet: The Nocturnal Forager

A Mysterious Denizen of the African Night
In the shadowy underbrush of Kenya and Tanzania, the African Civet (Civettictis civetta) emerges as a unique and enigmatic creature of the night. Known for its distinctive coat pattern and secretive lifestyle, the African Civet is one of the continent's most intriguing nocturnal mammals. This chapter uncovers the life of the African Civet, exploring its biology, behavior, and ecological significance in the African wild.

Physical Description and Characteristics
The African Civet is a medium-sized mammal, weighing between 7 to 20 kilograms (15 to 44 pounds). It possesses a stocky body with short legs and a long, bushy tail. The civet's most notable feature is its striking coat pattern, characterized by a greyish or brownish base color with a series of black bands, spots, and stripes. This patterning provides excellent camouflage in the dappled moonlight of their forest and savannah habitats. The civet also has a prominent crest of erectile hair along its spine, which can be raised as a display or when threatened.

Diet and Foraging Habits
African Civets are omnivorous, with a diet that includes small mammals, insects, birds, fruits, and carrion. They are opportunistic foragers, using their keen sense of smell to locate food. At night, they can be seen rummaging through the forest floor or in open areas, searching for a variety of foods to satisfy their varied diet.

Habitat and Distribution

The African Civet inhabits a range of environments, including forests, savannahs, and riverine habitats. They are well-adapted to both wooded and open areas, showing a preference for regions with dense underbrush or foliage where they can hide during the day.

Behavior and Lifestyle

African Civets are solitary and nocturnal animals, spending the day in burrows or dense vegetation. They are known to be excellent climbers and swimmers, although they spend most of their time on the ground. Civets mark their territory using a musky secretion from their perineal glands, which is also used in the perfume industry.

Reproduction and Offspring

The reproductive habits of the African Civet are not well-documented. However, it is known that they give birth to one to four offspring after a gestation period of around 60 to 70 days. The young are raised in dens and are cared for by the mother until they are old enough to fend for themselves.

Predation and Defense

The African Civet faces threats from larger predators such as leopards, hyenas, and pythons. Its primary defense mechanism is its agility and ability to secrete a foul-smelling substance from its anal glands, which deters predators and marks its territory.

Threats and Conservation

While African Civets are not currently endangered, they face threats from habitat destruction and hunting for their musk and fur. Their adaptability to different environments has helped them maintain stable populations, but conservation efforts are needed to ensure their continued survival.

The African Civet in Culture

In some African cultures, the African Civet is regarded with a mixture of fascination and wariness due to its nocturnal habits and distinctive appearance. It sometimes features in folklore and traditional medicine.

Ecological Role

As omnivores, African Civets play a crucial role in their ecosystems. They help control populations of rodents and insects and contribute to seed dispersal through their fruit-eating habits. Understanding the ecological role of the African Civet is essential for conserving the biodiversity of their habitats.

The Servaline Genet: Kenya's Elusive Carnivore

A Shadowy Figure of the African Night
In the dense forests and bushlands of Kenya, the Servaline Genet (Genetta servalina) moves with stealth and grace. This small, elusive carnivore, part of the Viverridae family, is a lesser-known yet fascinating inhabitant of the African wild. This chapter uncovers the secretive world of the Servaline Genet, discussing its physical attributes, behavior, diet, and the role it plays in its natural habitat.

Physical Description and Characteristics
The Servaline Genet is a slender, cat-like animal with a long body and tail. It typically weighs between 1.5 to 2 kilograms (3.3 to 4.4 pounds) and measures up to 90 centimeters (35 inches) in length, including the tail. The genet's coat is golden or buff-colored with a series of black spots and stripes, which provide camouflage in the dappled light of the forest. It has a small head with large ears and eyes, adapted for nocturnal living. The long, bushy tail is marked with rings and helps in balance.

Habitat and Distribution
Servaline Genets are primarily found in the forests and dense bushlands of Central and East Africa, with a notable presence in Kenya. They prefer habitats with dense vegetation that offer ample hiding spots and hunting grounds. These genets are arboreal, spending much of their time in trees.

Diet and Feeding Habits

As carnivores, Servaline Genets primarily feed on small mammals, birds, insects, and occasionally fruits. They are adept hunters, using their agility and stealth to catch prey. Their diet plays a crucial role in controlling the population of rodents and other small animals in their ecosystem.

Behavior and Lifestyle

Servaline Genets are solitary and nocturnal creatures, most active during the night when they hunt and explore their territory. They are known for their agile movements and can leap and climb with ease. During the day, they rest in tree hollows, dense foliage, or other secluded spots.

Reproduction and Offspring

Little is known about the reproductive habits of the Servaline Genet in the wild. Like other genet species, they are likely polygynous, with males mating with multiple females. The female genet gives birth to a small litter of one to three young after a gestation period of around 70 to 77 days. The young are cared for in a secure den, often in a hollow tree or a similar sheltered location.

Predation and Defense Mechanisms

The main predators of the Servaline Genet include larger mammals and birds of prey. When threatened, genets rely on their agility and climbing skills to escape danger. They are also known to emit a strong odor from their anal glands as a defense mechanism.

Threats and Conservation

The primary threats to the Servaline Genet include habitat destruction due to deforestation and human expansion, as well as trapping and hunting. While their elusive nature makes it difficult to determine their exact population status, conservation efforts focus on habitat preservation and reducing human-wildlife conflict.

The Servaline Genet in African Culture

In local cultures, genets are often surrounded by mystery due to their nocturnal habits and elusive nature. They are sometimes featured in folklore and are respected for their agility and stealth.

Ecological Role

The Servaline Genet plays an important role in its ecosystem as a predator. By controlling the populations of small mammals and insects, they help maintain the ecological balance in their habitats. Studying these animals provides valuable insights into the health and dynamics of forest and bushland ecosystems in Kenya.

Epilogue: Reflections on Kenya and Tanzania's Wildlife Tapestry

As we draw this exploration of Kenya and Tanzania's remarkable wildlife to a close, it is fitting to reflect on the intricate and vibrant tapestry that these animals weave in the ecosystem. Each species, from the majestic lions and elephants to the elusive genets and civets, plays a crucial role in maintaining the ecological balance and health of these diverse habitats.

The chapters of this book have taken us on a journey through the savannahs, forests, and waterways, introducing us to the inhabitants of these landscapes. We have seen the power and grace of the big cats, the gentle giants of the plains, and the smaller, often overlooked creatures that contribute just as significantly to the ecological diversity of the region.

Interconnectedness of Species

One key insight is the interconnectedness of all these species. The predatory prowess of the lion influences the behavior of herbivores, which in turn affects the vegetation patterns of the savannah. The foraging habits of elephants create microhabitats for other species, and the burrowing of aardvarks and other small mammals improves soil quality and aids in seed dispersal.

Challenges and Threats
However, this rich tapestry is under threat. Habitat loss, climate change, poaching, and human-wildlife conflict are just some of the challenges these animals face. The decline of one species can have cascading effects on the entire ecosystem. The plight of the African elephant and rhinoceros, heavily targeted by poachers, is a stark reminder of the fragility of this balance.

Conservation Efforts
This book has also highlighted the numerous conservation efforts underway to protect these species and their habitats. National parks and reserves in Kenya and Tanzania, such as the Serengeti, Maasai Mara, and Ngorongoro Crater, are crucial bastions of biodiversity. Conservationists, researchers, and local communities are working tirelessly to find sustainable solutions to protect these natural treasures.

The Role of Education and Awareness
Education and awareness are paramount in conservation efforts. By understanding the behavior, needs, and challenges of each species, we can better appreciate their place in the ecosystem. This book aims not only to inform but also to inspire a sense of wonder and a deep respect for these creatures and their environments.

Looking to the Future
Looking forward, the future of Kenya and Tanzania's wildlife hinges on a delicate balance of conservation, sustainable development, and community involvement. It is a future that requires us to recognize the intrinsic value of each species, no matter how small or inconspicuous. We hold the key to ensuring that future generations will have the opportunity to marvel at these creatures in their natural habitats, just as we have.

In closing, the wildlife of Kenya and Tanzania is a testament to nature's beauty, resilience, and complexity. It is a world that demands our respect, awe, and steadfast commitment to preservation. As stewards of the Earth, it is our responsibility to protect and cherish this extraordinary legacy.

Printed in Great Britain
by Amazon